Macbook for Seniors: The Most Easy-to-Follow and Intuitive Guide to Master Your MacBook Air and Pro. Best Tips and Tricks and Instructions for Senior Beginner User Included

CONTENTS:

Introduction 3

Chapter 1: How to Set Up your MacBook 4

    1.1 MacBook Overview 4

    1.2 Using the Trackpad and Keyboard 5

    1.3 Use Login Screen and Touch ID on Mac 6

    1.4 Desktop Settings 9

    1.5 How to work with File and Folders 17

    1.6 Menu Bar 20

    1.7 Connecting to Wi-Fi Network 26

Chapter 2: The Basics of the Mac 28

    2.1 Basic Settings 28

    2.2 Work with Documents 34

    2.3 Adding an Email Account on your Mac 37

    2.4 Media files 39

        Photos 39

        Videos 45

        Books 49

        Music 51

    2.5 Use iCloud 54

    2.6 Control Center 60

    2.7 Notifications & Widget 61

    2.8 Use Apple Pay 64

Chapter 3: Using the Internet 66

    3.1 Using Safari and other browsers 66

3.2 Navigate the Internet 70

3.3 Downloading Files 72

3.5 Best Websites for Seniors 75

Chapter 4: Essential and Popular Apps 78

4.1 AppStore and Installing Apps 78

4.2 Launching an Application on Mac 82

4.3 Closing and Uninstalling an Application on Mac 84

4.4 Mostly used Apps 87

Chapter 5: Troubleshooting, Tips, and Tricks for Seniors 97

5.1 Use your Mac with other devices 97

5.2 Talk to Siri...99

5.3 Back up your Files..101

5.4 The Genius Bar for Troubleshooting your Mac 110

Bonus: Mac Keyboard Shortcut 114

Conclusion 122

Introduction

Using a Mac is straightforward. In fact, they are regarded as more user-friendly than Windows computers. But there is a learning curve if you've never used one before, especially if you're accustomed to Windows.

In this guide for Mac users, we will cover the fundamentals needed to get started. From navigating the operating system to identifying and resolving any issues.

Chapter 1: How to Set Up your MacBook

1.1 MacBook Overview

Apple's MacBook is a family of Macintosh-based laptop computers. The MacBook series includes the MacBook (2006-present), the MacBook Pro (2006-present), and the MacBook Air (2008-present).

As Apple shifted to using Intel instead of PowerPC processors, the PowerBook and iBook product lines merged to form the MacBook portfolio.

MacBook

From late 2011 through 2014, the manufacture of the original MacBook ended, but it was reintroduced at the start of 2015. The 2015 model, known by titles such as "New MacBook" and "MacBook Retina", had several essential improvements.

The Force Touch trackpad and a butterfly mechanism for the keyboard's switches were two advances.

Apple MacBook Pro

The MacBook Pro, sometimes known as the MBP, is a somewhat thicker and potentially more significant notebook than the MacBook. It is designed for customers that require their laptop to handle more heavy jobs, such as video editing, because of its more robust internals. The MacBook Pro was the first Apple notebook to include Apple's proprietary Thunderbolt connector in 2011.

Macintosh Air

The MacBook Air was marketed as a more affordable and portable alternative to the MacBook. Therefore, the MacBook Air is the only model without a Retina Display option. When it debuted in January 2008, the MacBook Air was the smallest and lightest member of the MacBook family.

1.2 Using the Trackpad and Keyboard

Mac users lack the ability to handle several computers with a single keyboard and mouse, unlike Windows PC users. Universal Control enables users of macOS and iPadOS to share the same cursor, mouse, trackpad, and keyboard across a Mac and an iPad. Additionally, if you have many Macs or iPads, you may share these controls across them.

Universal Control is presently labeled as a beta feature by Apple, although it appears stable enough to use without issue. This capability is distinct from Sidecar, which allows you to utilize an iPad as a second monitor at home. Only Universal Control permits the independent usage of various devices with the same input modalities.

Universal Control Compatibility

Your devices must satisfy specific prerequisites for this to operate. Your iPad must run iPadOS 15.4 or later, and your Mac must have macOS Monterey 12.0 or later. Additionally, your device must be one of the following:

- MacBook Pro debuted later than in 2016
- Apple MacBook Air models released in 2018 or later

- Mac mini debuted later than 2018
- iMac launched in 2017 or after, in addition to iMac (Retina 5K, 27-inch, Late 2015)
- iMac Pro was released in 2017.
- Mac Pro introduced later than 2019

Using two-factor authentication, you must sign in to each device with the same Apple ID and password. With Bluetooth, Wi-Fi, and Handoff enabled, each device must be within 30 feet of the other. For this to operate, your Mac or cellular-enabled iPad cannot be sharing its internet connection. Now, let's see how everything plays out.

1.3 Use Login Screen and Touch ID on Mac

Numerous individuals view passwords as inadequate for security. The first step is to recall them. The only method to guarantee that you will not forget or lose your password is to write it down and keep the paper (or another medium) secure.

If you have a modern MacBook Pro or MacBook Air that supports Touch ID, there is a better method. Instead of a password, Touch ID allows you to use your fingerprint. Touch ID will unlock your Mac, but it is also secure enough to provide access to Apple Pay and other Apple services involving money.

Touch ID is not a complete replacement for passwords. After restarting your Mac, you will need to enter your password. After entering your password to log in, you may utilize Touch ID.

To utilize Touch ID, you must set it up (often a one-time operation) and be ready to use it whenever you like.

How to configure Touch ID

1. Setting up Touch ID on your Mac is a straightforward, one-time operation that requires only a few steps.
2. Dry your hands after washing them. Wet hands are incompatible with Touch ID.
3. Select AppleSystem Preferences from the menu. Displays the System Preferences window.

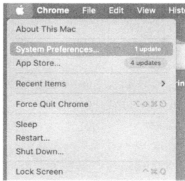

4. Tap Touch ID in the System Preferences window.

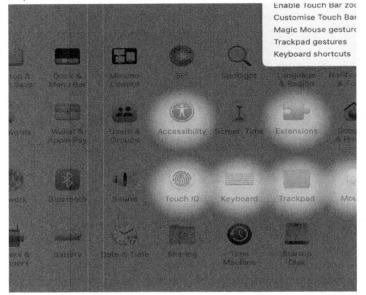

5. To add a fingerprint, click +. You are prompted for your password.

6. Provide your password.

7. Select the Touch ID capabilities you wish to employ on your MacBook. Your selections are:

8. Activating your Mac

9. Paying using Apple Pay on iTunes and the App Store

10. Follow the procedures for fingerprint registration.

You must gently press your finger on the Touch ID button and hold it there until registration is complete and you are directed to use another finger. You must register several fingerprints to finish the procedure.

1.4 Desktop Settings

Due to Apple's security safeguards, it is impossible to customize your Mac with extensive system modifications. However, there are further methods to personalize your macOS desktop. Therefore, let's examine how to personalize your Mac desktop in seven simple actions.

1. Begin With a Fresh Wallpaper

Simply replacing the default wallpaper with one of your choosing will revitalize your desktop.

To make this little adjustment, launch System Preferences and choose Desktop & Screen Saver.

Choose a new picture from the default Mac desktop themes under the Desktop menu, or opt for a solid backdrop color. In addition, don't forget to check out the Dynamic Desktop area, which features wallpapers that vary according to the time of day.

You may also browse your Photos library from the sidebar to set your background to an image you enjoy and don't mind seeing daily.

To view different wallpapers from an album, check the Change picture box and select a time interval, such as Every 5 minutes.

2. Create a Unique Color Scheme

Your Mac enables you to mix and match several color settings for system accents and highlights to create your own color scheme. To do so, navigate to System Preferences > General and select new accents and highlight colors.

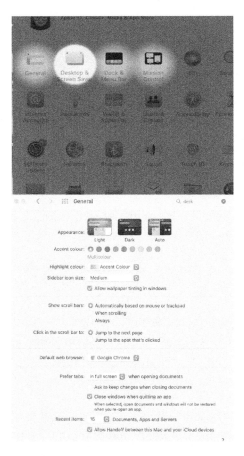

The altered color scheme will then be mirrored across buttons, boxes, menus, and other system elements.

Alternately, under the same preferences box as above, there is an option to switch to Dark Mode (just after the light one). It is available on all Macs running macOS Mojave or later and provides the Dock, menu bar, program windows, and sidebars with a sleek, black design.

Since you cannot apply system-wide themes to your Mac, you should enable app-specific themes instead. For instance, if you use Alfred to operate your Mac and have enabled the Powerpack, you may modify Alfred's appearance using a custom theme, as outlined on the Alfred Support website.

3. Include Personality-Rich Icons and Backgrounds

In Finder, you can not only resize icons (Select View > Show View Options > Icon size from the menu) but also alter their appearance using custom icons.

Stack By: None   ⌃⌄

Sort By: None   ⌃⌄

Icon size: 64×64

Grid spacing:

Text size: 12   ⌃⌄

Label position:

● Bottom   ◯ Right

☐ Show item info

✓ Show icon preview

When searching for icons in online repositories, don't forget to look for the ICNS extension (which ensures compatibility with macOS). PNGs and JPGs can also function as icon sources, however, ICNS images that are compatible with macOS are preferable.

To change the icon of a folder (or a file), you must first copy the new icon file (select it and press Cmd + C). Select the folder whose icon you wish to alter, then navigate to File > Get Info.

Select the icon at the top of the inspector window and select Edit > Paste or press Cmd + V. Your personalized icon should now be present. Select it in the inspector and press the Delete key to revert to the default icon if you're not satisfied.

You may even utilize an existing icon as the image source by copying it from the corresponding inspector. Here's a screenshot of the icon for the Music library folder, which has the Apple Music app icon.

Want to replace the default application icons in the Applications folder with your own? Except for the applications that come pre-installed on your Mac, you may do so for everything. However, utilizing the icons of system programs as sources for third-party apps poses no difficulty. You may, for instance, replace the symbol for your preferred third-party web browser with the system icon for Safari.

4. Redesign the Login Page

To customize the login screen on your Mac, begin by changing your account's user image. This is possible via System Preferences > Users & Groups. Select your user account and ensure that the Password tab is selected.

Click the existing user image next to your username to replace it with one from Apple's default collection or your Photos library. Even a Memoji or an Animoji can be substituted. To put the selected image, click Save.

Next, you should consider creating an amusing lock screen message. To do so, navigate to System Preferences > Security & Privacy > General and choose the Show a notification when the screen is locked checkbox.

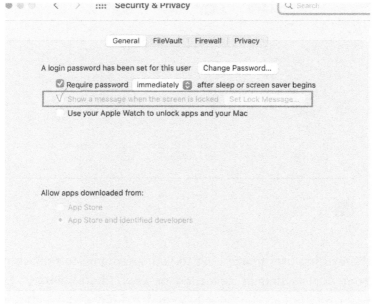

If the option is unavailable, you must click the Lock symbol at the bottom of the pane and enter the system password when requested. Then, you should be able to begin altering it.

Next, select the Set Lock Message option, enter the desired message for the lock screen, and click OK. When you restart your Mac, the notification will appear just above the power options at the bottom of the screen.

5. Get a Better-Looking Dock

To customize the Dock on your Mac, you should at the very least clear it. Remove the icons of seldom-used applications by dragging them out and releasing them when the Remove icon appears. Then, drag your preferred applications from the Applications folder to the Dock.

While hovering, you may also rotate the Dock, resize its icons, and alter their magnification to varying degrees. To access these changes, navigate to System Preferences > Dock & Menu Bar. Alternately, use the following Terminal commands to personalize Dock.

In addition, rather than tinkering with the Dock, you might replace it with a third-party customization option such as uBar.

6. Redesign Individual Applications

To add additional personal touches to your Mac, experiment with the default settings of installed applications. If you have the Slack desktop software installed, for instance, you may customize the Slack sidebar with a new layout.

Change the appearance of your emails in the Mac Mail application

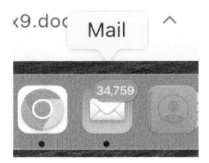

by adjusting the fonts and colors by navigating to Preferences > Fonts & Colors. In addition, you may highlight certain messages by choosing them and selecting a different color from Format > Show Colors.

Additionally, you may obtain fresh skin for the Terminal via Preferences > Profiles when it is open. Select one of the available themes in the sidebar and click Default to make it the default. The terminal must be restarted for the new color profile to take effect.

If you're a fan of dark mode, why not enable it in your favorite Mac applications? Numerous applications, including Ulysses, Bear, Things, Tweetbot, and Spark, enable darker themes.

7. Add Custom Sound Effects to Mac

You need not restrict your customization efforts to cosmetic modifications. How about adding some audio adjustments? In System Preferences > Accessibility > Spoken Content > System Voice, you can select a different system voice as the default. Select a new notification sound from System Preferences > Sound > Sound Effects.

In System Preferences > Date & Time > Clock, you may configure your Mac to announce the time at predetermined intervals.

As you can see, with little thought, work, and effort, you can genuinely personalize your Mac. After doing so, it will be much more pleasing to look at and work with. After making all of Instead of those cosmetic adjustments, why not focus on making your Mac more user-friendly for everyday tasks?

1.5 How to work with File and Folders

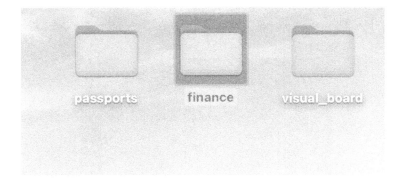

Photos, text documents, and video clips may be stored quickly and easily on a brand-new Mac desktop. As the number of files accumulates, searching for files may become more time-consuming over time. Folders are the answer. Similar to a traditional paper folder, relevant files can be gathered and saved in a single location. In addition, files within a folder can be organized based on certain criteria. Learn how to quickly create, rename, and modify folders on your Mac.

Creating a new folder on macOS is more than a simple procedure.

Every Mac includes pre-installed folders for file management. Included are the Applications, Documents, and Downloads folders in the macOS "Finder" file manager. When you download new fonts for your Mac from the web, for instance, the files are immediately saved in the Downloads folder. On macOS, there are also hidden folders containing crucial system files. If you wish to arrange your data by creating folders on your iMac or MacBook, you have numerous alternatives. Examine all three to see which one best matches your own workflow.

Create a folder on a Mac: option 1

- Go to your Mac's desktop.
- Tap the trackpad with two fingers close together on a MacBook.

- Once the menu displays, click the "New Folder" option. In a few seconds, the new folder should be added to the desktop.

Create a folder on a Mac: option 2

- Go to your Mac's desktop.
- Enter the following keystroke sequence on your keyboard: ⌘ + Shift + N
- The new folder will appear on your desktop in a few seconds.

Before you can organize your files into folders based on certain criteria, you must rename the newly created folder. This may be accomplished by double-clicking the new folder. The title will be emphasized, and its appearance can be altered as desired. Alternatively, you may just right-click on the folder to bring up a menu on your desktop. To make changes, pick the "Rename" option. You are permitted to alter the name of your folder whenever necessary.

Simply drag the relevant files into the corresponding folder to add them to your folder. To accomplish this, hold down the left mouse button until the folder is highlighted in blue. Additionally, you may drag the files into the folder window. Using the choices shown above, you may create subfolders within your folder.

To rename the folder you need to tap the touchpad with two fingers at once . Then simply choose the "rename"button.

In each folder, any number of subfolders can be created.

Delete folders or individual files by dragging and dropping them into the trash bin in the lower-right corner of the Dock bar. You may alternatively right-click the folder or file to bring up a menu, then pick "Move to Trash" from the menu. If you have accidentally erased a folder, you can also recover your Mac data.

1.6 Menu Bar

MacOS is supposed to be user-friendly for the ordinary computer user, yet locating some tools and functions can be difficult, especially when using System Preferences. Fortunately, Mac's menu bar (the thin strip at the top of the screen) has extremely handy shortcuts to the most essential functionalities.

What's on the menu bar on Mac?

The easiest way to utilize the menu bar on a Mac is to become familiar with its contents.

- **Apple menu** - This is where you will find important system tools and features, such as information about your Mac, System Preferences, access to the App Store (and whether app updates are available), recently opened items, and a shortcut for putting your Mac to sleep, restarting your Mac, shutting down your Mac, and logging out of your account.

▢ **App menu** - Immediately below the Apple menu symbol is the presently chosen app menu. When an application is active and in use, you will find categories such as File, Edit, View, Window, and Help. Each application has a unique menu layout.

▢ **System status menu** - The System status menu contains widgets from the Mac App Store, volume controls, Wi-Fi status, AirPlay, the battery (on laptops), and the date.

▢ **Spotlight** is Mac's system-wide and web-based search engine. You may enter anything into Spotlight's search bar, and you will almost certainly discover what you're looking for. You can open it by pressing the command+space button.

Q Spotlight Search

▢ **Siri** - With Siri on the Mac, the personal digital assistant may be used to seek up information, add appointments to the calendar, and make reminders, among other things.
To open Siri:

1)Tap Siri in the Touch Bar (if your Mac has a Touch Bar).

2)Say "Hey Siri" (if enabled in Siri preferences; this option's only available when supported by your Mac, display or headphones).

3)search siri in spotlight

☐ **Notification Center** - You may configure widgets in Notification Center to offer quick access to the things that are most important to you, including the weather, your daily schedule, iTunes control, and exclusive content from some third-party apps.

How to delete widgets from the Mac menu bar?

Over time, the menu bar can get congested, especially when third-party widgets are added. If you do not use macOS status widgets, you can delete them.

☐ Control-click or right-click on a Menu bar widget.
☐ Select Open Settings.
☐ Uncheck the Show in the Menu bar box.

When you click on the widget in third-party applications (such as Fantastical 2), there is typically a settings icon (that looks like a gear) that you may click to deactivate or disable menu bar access.

How to change the date and the time in the menu bar on the Mac?

Change the date, time, time zone, and appearance of your Mac's Date & Time.

Caution: If you manually change the date and time on your Mac, you may have detrimental effects on apps running on your computer and may be banned from certain games that consider time changes a form of cheating.

How to change the date and time manually

1. Click the date and time in the menu bar located in the upper-right corner of the screen.
2. Click on the link labeled "Open Date & Time Preferences."
3. Select the Time & Date tab.

4. To make modifications, click the lock.
5. Click Unlock after entering your administrator password.
6. Uncheck the option labeled Automatically set date and time.
7. Choose a new date.
8. Choose a new time.
9. You may also automatically set the date and time for a different nation. You can select the United States, Asia, or Europe.

How to change the time zone manually

☐ Click the date and time in the menu bar located in the upper-right corner of the screen.
☐ Click on the link labeled "Open Date & Time Preferences."
☐ Select the Time Zone button.
☐ To make modifications, click the lock.
☐ Click Unlock after entering your administrator password.
☐ Uncheck the option next to Set time zone automatically based on location.

- Click a different area.
- How to alter the appearance of the date and time Menu bar widget
- Click the date and time in the Menu bar located in the upper-right corner of the screen.
- Click on the link labeled Open Date & Time Preferences.
- Select the Time tab.
- To make modifications, click the lock.
- Click Unlock after entering your administrator password.
- Click Digital or Analog to modify the appearance of the clock.
- To display the day of the week, check the box next to Show the day of the week.
- Check the box next to Show date to display the date.

How to use the battery icon in the Mac menu bar?

The battery widget in the menu bar, which is exclusive to Apple computers, displays the remaining battery life before you must recharge. It also displays a few interesting statistics regarding your usage.

1. Select the battery icon.

2. The first status indicates approximately how much time remains until the battery dies. In addition, it displays whether your laptop is using battery power or is hooked up to an outlet.
3. The second status indicates which application is draining the battery. This is useful if you observe that your battery is depleting much faster than usual. It may be an app with bugs.
4. Click Show Percentage to display the remaining battery power as a percentage.

5. Click the Open Energy Saver Preferences button to configure the amount of time your screen and hard drive remain active while not in use.

How to use the spotlight on a Mac?

Spotlight is Apple's system-wide search tool. It will search for applications, documents, files, emails, and more when you enter a search phrase. It also searches the internet, contacts, and maps for directions, converts currencies, performs computations, and much more. It is a one-stop shop for all the shortcuts you use on your Mac.

How to make use of Siri on a Mac?

Siri on the Mac, like Siri on the iPhone and iPad, may serve as your own virtual assistant. It searches for files and folders on your Mac, arranges calendar events, and stores significant search results in your Notification Center. Want to learn something? Siri can assist with this.

How to use the notification center on the Mac?

The Notification Center is a side panel that you may visit whenever you want to quickly view today's schedule, the weather forecast for the afternoon, or your to-do list. Using third-party Notification Center widgets, you may customize your Today display with your most essential productivity applications.

How to change the menu bar icon order?

☐ Depress the command key on the keyboard.

- ⬚ Click on the symbol you wish to relocate. Ensure that the command button is still depressed.
- ⬚ Drag the symbol to its new spot by dragging it.
- ⬚ Release the mouse and command key to allow the icon to drop into place.

BONUS: PRO TIPS FOR MENU BAR WIDGETS ON THE MAC

When the option key is pressed on the keyboard while clicking on certain menu bar widgets, alternative information is displayed.

- ⬚ Option + Click on Wi-Fi to get further information about your wireless network, including your IP address, the address of your router, and your security type. Additionally, you may generate a diagnostic report and launch a wireless diagnostic.
- ⬚ Option + Click on Bluetooth to view further information on your Bluetooth connection, including its address and version. On your desktop, you may also write a diagnostic report.
- ⬚ Option + Click Notification Center to manually enable or off Do Not Disturb.

1.7 Connecting to Wi-Fi Network

Before connecting to your Wi-Fi, the following must be understood:

- ⬚ Wi-Fi name (SSID)
- ⬚ Wi-Fi security key, password, or passphrase

Step 1: Click on the AirPort/Wi-Fi icon on the desktop, then pick the Wi-Fi name (SSID) to which you wish to connect.

- ⬚ Enter the Wi-Fi password when prompted, then click Join.

- ▢ Check the Remember this network option if you want your Mac computer to remember this Wi-Fi network and connect to it automatically when it is within range.
- ▢ When this icon appears in the menu bar, it indicates a successful connection.
- ▢ Utilizing the Network pane to connect

Step 2: On the desktop, pick the System Preferences... option by clicking the Apple symbol.

Click the Network icon in Step 2.

Step 3: Pick Wi-Fi from the left pane, click the Network Name drop-down menu and then select the Wi-Fi network name to which you wish to join.

NOTE: Depending on the version of your Mac, Wi-Fi may appear as AirPort. Enter the Wi-Fi password when prompted, then click Join. Check the Remember this network option if you want your Mac computer to remember this Wi-Fi network and connect to it automatically when it is within range.

Step 4: Click "Apply."

You should now be connected to the Wi-Fi successfully.

Chapter 2: The Basics of the Mac

2.1 Basic Settings

While unboxing a brand-new MacBook is definitely thrilling, there are a number of changes, recommendations, and repairs you should perform on Day 1 that go beyond the default MacBook settings. Here are some of my favorite applications that will make your smartphone easier to use.

After you've navigated through the early stages of the Mac Setup Assistant, when you're prompted to enter your Apple ID, connect to a network, etc., consider updating or at least reviewing these settings on your new MacBook.

Check for amendments

Has Apple released a macOS upgrade since it manufactured your MacBook? Click the Apple icon in the upper-left corner of the screen and choose About This Mac to find out. You should be viewing the General tab inside About This Mac. In this case, click the Software Update icon to access System Preferences and check for updates.

Enhanced battery charging

If your MacBook will spend the majority of its time plugged in, you should adjust this setting. MacOS may learn your charging patterns to extend the life of your battery. Select Battery Preferences from the drop-down menu that appears when you click the battery symbol in the menu bar at the top of your display. (If you don't see a battery icon in the menu bar, go to System Preferences > Energy Saver and choose

Show battery status in the menu bar.) Select Optimized battery charging at the bottom of the available selections. This will delay charging after the battery reaches 80% capacity.

Set up Siri

By default, Siri should be activated, but if you wish to use Siri just on your iPhone, you may disable Siri by navigating to System Preferences > Siri and deselecting the Enable Ask Siri checkbox. If you want to use Siri regularly, you may customize Siri's voice, language, and keyboard shortcuts from this window.

Modify the Touch Bar

If you have one of the final remaining Intel-based MacBook Pro models with the Touch Bar, navigate to System Preferences > Keyboard, select the Customize Touch Bar option, and then drag the buttons you wish to appear on the Touch Bar's default view to the Touch Bar below the display. Not to fear, they will traverse the hinge from your display to the Touch Bar.

Sync directories through iCloud

Syncing the Desktop and Documents folders between my two Macs and my iOS devices is really beneficial. To synchronize these two folders, navigate to System Preferences > Apple ID > iCloud and select the box next to iCloud Drive. Select the Desktop and Documents directories by clicking Options next to iCloud Drive and then selecting the Desktop and Documents folders.

Choose default browser

Even though Chrome consumes more system resources than Safari, I prefer it since the favicons make it easier to monitor all of my open tabs. To change the default web browser, navigate to System Preferences > General and pick an alternative to Safari as the default web browser.

Set the direction of the scrolling

The "normal" scrolling direction of a MacBook does not feel natural to me. If you wish the two-finger swipe gesture to scroll vertically in the other direction, select the Scroll & Zoom option in System Preferences > Trackpad. Uncheck the item labeled "Scroll direction: Natural next."

Insert and delete objects from the Dock

Apple places a number of default applications in the Dock at the bottom of the display. You may create room in the Dock for the apps you use most frequently by deleting unnecessary ones. To remove an app from the Dock, click and drag its icon to the desktop until the word Remove appears above the icon, and then release. Voila, it has vanished! To add an application to the Dock, launch it and then right-click on its Dock icon, hover over the Options line, and select Keep in Dock.

Shift the Dock

On a widescreen MacBook display, you may find it more useful to have the Dock on the side rather than at the bottom of the screen. To relocate the Dock, choose Left or Right for Position on Screen in System Preferences > Dock & Menu Bar. While there, you can also modify the size of the Dock by dragging a slider. Checking the box to Automatically hide and reveal the Dock will also cause it to disappear while it is not in use.

Display battery percent

Similar to an iPhone, a MacBook shows a little battery symbol at the top of the screen to indicate the remaining battery life. It would be more useful if the remaining battery % was also displayed next to this symbol. To display the percentage, navigate to System Preferences > Dock & Menu Bar > Battery on the left. Check the box next to Show Percentage, and the percentage should appear in the Menu Bar next to the battery indicator.

Stop autoplaying videos

Safari now combats two of the most irritating aspects of the Internet: autoplay videos and ad trackers. Ad tracking is disabled by default, however, you will need to enable a global setting to prevent autoplay videos.

Click on the Websites tab under Safari's Preferences. Select Auto-Play from the menu on the left and Select Never Auto-Play or Stop Media with Sound at the bottom of the window while browsing other websites and enjoy the silence.

Perform a Night Shift

Before bed, staring at a blue screen might disrupt your body's internal schedule and make it harder to fall asleep. With Apple's Night Move function, your display's colors shift toward the warmer end of the color spectrum in the evening. Click the Night Shift tab inside System Preferences > Displays. You may configure Night Shift to activate from sunset to sunrise, or you can choose a custom time range. Use the slider to modify the effect's color temperature between less and more warmth. Once you begin using Night Shift, you will wonder how you ever endured evenings in front of a frigid, blue screen.

Make your desktop dynamic

Apple created a dynamic wallpaper for MacOS Mojave that gradually changes its lighting throughout the day, from a bright, sunny desert picture during the day to a cool, dark screen at night. Go to System Preferences > Desktop & Screen Saver to locate it. Although Mojave initially came with only two dynamic wallpapers, Mojave and Solar Gradients, there are now plenty to pick from and sites where you can download more ones.

Try the night mode

MacOS Mojave also included an authentic dark mode for Macs. Go to System Preferences > General to find the Light and Dark settings for Appearance at the top. On the majority of applications, dark mode makes the backdrop black and the text white.

Want both Light and Dark alternatives? When Auto is selected, the buttons, menus, and windows will alter throughout the day.

Set Do Not Disturb hours

Along with blue displays, alerts beyond a particular hour have no place in my household. As with iOS, macOS allows you to mute alerts at night so that you are not interrupted when watching Netflix or sleeping. Select the option labeled Turn on Do Not Disturb from System Preferences > Notifications. By default, the Do Not Disturb Window is set from 10 p.m. to 7 a.m., but you may customize it. There are choices to enable the function while the display of your MacBook is asleep or when you are mirroring the display to a TV or projector (and presumably watching a movie or show or video). You may also allow calls to come through (if you use your MacBook to accept calls) or merely repeated calls, which may indicate an emergency or anything that requires your immediate attention.

Set app download limit tolerability

If you want to download software from the entire web and not just the Mac App Store, you must instruct MacOS to loosen up a bit. To make changes, navigate to System Preferences > Security & Privacy > General, then click the lock in the lower-left corner and enter your password. Choose App Store and recognized developers under Allow applications to be downloaded from.

Select the rate at which your MacBook locks

On the Security & Privacy tab, you may configure how long your MacBook can be inactive before locking the screen. Setting a longer duration is more convenient, but less secure. You must also specify the amount of time before the screen saver begins, as the timer will not start until the screen saver is activated. By navigating to System

Preferences > Desktop & Screen Saver and using the drop-down menu at the top of the window, you can set the design and duration of your screen saver.

2.2 Work with Documents

You may generate reports, essays, spreadsheets, financial charts, presentations, and slideshows with macOS applications, such as Pages or TextEdit, or Mac App Store applications.

Tip: If you have concerns about how to use an application such as Pages or TextEdit, select Help from the menu bar while working on the application, then consult the application's user guide.

Create documents

On your Mac, launch a document-creation application (Pages for example).

- ☐ Open TextEdit to produce a plain text, rich text, or HTML document, for example.
- ☐ Click New Document in the Open dialogue box, or navigate to File > New.

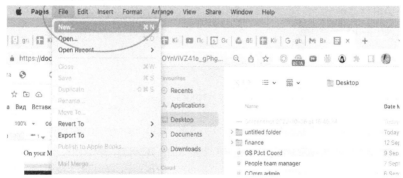

Numerous Mac machines include the following Apple applications for creating reports, spreadsheets, and presentations, among other things:

Create letters, reports, fliers, and posters, among other documents. Pages contain several document templates that make it simple to generate attractive papers. Consult the Pages User Manual.

Create spreadsheets to show and organize your data. Start with a template and alter it to your liking by adding formulae, charts, and photos, among other things. Consult the Numbers User Manual.

Create captivating presentations with photos, videos, charts, and slide animations with Keynote. Consult the Keynote User Manual.

If Pages, Numbers, or Keynote are not already installed on your Mac, you may download them from the App Store.

They are also accessible on iCloud.com and on iOS and iPadOS devices (through the App Store).

Format documents

There are several ways to format and manage text in documents on a Mac:

☐ Change fonts and styles by selecting Format > Show Fonts, Format > Font > Show Fonts, or Format > Style in a document. See Format text with typefaces in documents.

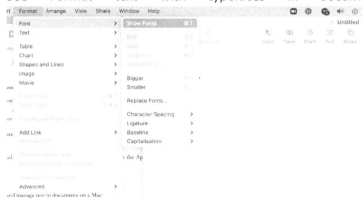

- ⬚ Change colors by selecting Format > Show Colors or Format > Font > Show Colors in a document. See Use colors in documents.
- ⬚ Enter many sorts of characters, including those with accent marks and diacritic markings.
- ⬚ In the majority of applications, spelling is checked as you enter, and errors are automatically rectified. You can disable these features or utilize other choices. See Check spelling and grammar.
- ⬚ Check definitions by selecting the desired text in a document, Control-clicking it, and selecting Look Up. See Look up words.
- ⬚ To translate text, pick the desired text in a document, Control-click it, and then select Translate. See Text translation.

Save documents

Many applications on your Mac will automatically save your papers as you work. You can save a document at any moment.

Save a document by selecting File > Save, entering a name, selecting where to save the document (click the down arrow to display more locations), and then click Save.

You may add tags to your saved documents to make them simpler to locate later. You may be able to save your document to iCloud Drive so that it is accessible on your desktops, iOS, and iPadOS devices with iCloud Drive installed.

Save a document under a different name: Choose File > Save As in a document, then input a new name. If Save As is not shown, hit and hold Option, then reopen the File menu.

Save a document as a copy: Choose File > Duplicate or File > Save As in a document.

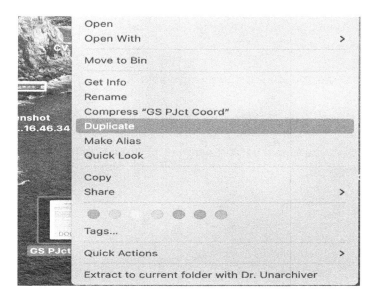

Additionally, you may save a document as a PDF and merge multiple files into a single PDF.

2.3 Adding an Email Account on your Mac

Apple's Mail is Apple's application for sending emails. Mail is integrated with macOS, so the application may be found on any Mac. The identical software is also available for your iPad and iPhone. It is an excellent alternative to utilizing a web browser to access your multiple email accounts, including Gmail and iCloud mail. In fact, one of the nicest features of Mail is that you can configure it to receive emails from all of your email accounts in one location, so you only need to use one app and you will never miss another email.

This chapter describes the procedures necessary to configure email on your Mac or MacBook, including how to establish a second email account.

As an introduction, we will highlight a few of the reasons why we use Mail on our Macs.

Here are some advantages of utilizing email:

- ⬜ You configure Mail to receive emails from all of your email addresses, including your business email and personal email, so that you can read and send all of your emails from the same location.

- ⬜ It is really simple to set up because it is compatible with popular email services such as Gmail, Yahoo! Mail, Outlook, and, of course, Apple's iCloud. It supports Exchange as well.
- ⬜ You may add and annotate attachments; for instance, you can email a photo or PDF with "drawn on" instructions.
- ⬜ It is compatible with other macOS applications, like Calendar and Maps.
- ⬜ Apple's Mail program will automatically offer the receiver a download link when you send huge files and folders as attachments.
- ⬜ It is really straightforward to block senders and unsubscribe from mailing lists.
- ⬜ When group interactions become too distracting, you may silence them.
- ⬜ You may organize your email messages into Mailboxes that adhere to specific parameters, such as unread, received today, or from specific individuals.
- ⬜ You may Flag your communications with a distinct color to make it simpler to locate certain groupings of emails.
- ⬜ It is simple to search through your whole email inbox.

To locate the Mail application on a Mac or MacBook, press Command + Space Bar and begin typing Mail, or select the Mail icon in the Dock.

How to configure Mail on a Mac

Setting up email on a Mac or MacBook is quite simple, especially if you use one of the more popular providers, such as Gmail, Yahoo, or Apple's iCloud. Only your email address and login credentials are required. Here is what must be done:

- Open System Preferences
- Select Internet Accounts.
- You'll see a list of frequently used services on the right, including iCloud, Exchange, Google, Twitter, Facebook, and Yahoo. If you do not see them, please click the plus symbol.

You may also add an email account from within Apple Mail; in fact, the program will encourage you to do so the first time you launch Mail.

- Open Mail.
- Click on Mail in the menu and select Accounts; this will open the same window as accessed via System Preferences.
- If you desire to disconnect or disable any of these accounts, simply pick them and click the minus (-) button on this page.

2.4 Media files

Photos

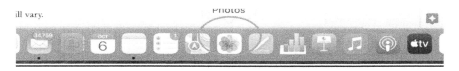

Apple's Photos for Mac has expanded upon the solid foundations established by iPhoto and Photos for iOS to provide you with a quick and practical method to organize, edit, and share all your photographs (without any stress).

In addition, using the Markup editor, you can be quite creative with your memories and design great things!

Whether you're new to photo management apps, upgrading from iPhoto, or researching alternatives to Aperture and Lightroom, here's all you need to know about Photos for macOS!

Starting off with Photos on a Mac

When you initially launch Photos, you are shown an overview of what the app will look like once you've uploaded all of your photos, videos, and memories. You will receive an overview of what to anticipate.

With the Photos app, you can create physical mementos such as calendars, collages, mugs, and more. However, these options are only accessible in the United States, Canada, Japan, and some European and Pacific Asian nations.

The introduction will demonstrate how to arrange and classify your photographs.

Depending on whether you are new to picture management or a veteran iPhoto, Aperture, or Lightroom user, your next steps will vary.

If you're new to organizing pictures on a Mac, do you have folders of disorganized images cluttering your desktop? Have you never used iPhoto or Aperture, Apple's two Mac picture programs? Photos facilitate the transfer of material from your desktop and iPhone to Photos on your Mac and in the cloud.

Once you have completed the basic setup, you can begin by uploading photos and videos or by taking a tour. If you're inexperienced with photos, the tour is your best option!

Upon completion of the trip, you have the option of...

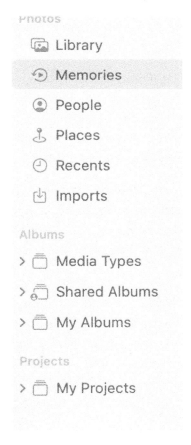

- Connect a camera or memory card to a computer
- Directly drag images into Photos
- Import is accessible via the file menu.
- Enable iCloud Photo Library in the Preferences menu.

... and with that, you are ready to begin uploading photographs!

If you're an iPhoto or Aperture upgrader

Aperture is incompatible with macOS Catalina as of now. You will still be able to use Photos to choose your Aperture library, as seen below, although this may only display the original images and not your adjustments. Apple will release a macOS Catalina update that addresses this vulnerability. You should maintain your Aperture library until then and plan to move it to Photos again.

Apple stated in 2014 that iPhoto and Aperture, its older picture storing and editing tools for the Mac, will no longer get updates. Instead, the company introduced Photos. If you've been fighting the change, but have now chosen to make the switch to Photos on the Mac, you won't experience as much agony as you may anticipate.

If you just have a single iPhoto library on your Mac, the Photos application should upgrade immediately when you launch it. If you need to utilize iPhoto for whatever reason, your old iPhoto library will remain, but updates made to older photographs will not immediately sync with your new photo library.

If you have numerous libraries on your computer, Photos will prompt you to choose which library to import. Unfortunately, many libraries cannot be merged into a single photo library; you must choose which one to use. If this is necessary, you can utilize Aperture to combine libraries and then import the consolidated library into Photos. However, importing an existing Aperture library into Photos is only possible through a manual migration.

Importing pictures and folders into Photos

After setting up Photos, the following step is to import your photos.

What you need to know about importing older photos and libraries into Photos for Mac.

- ☐ Launch Photos from the Dock or Applications directory.
- ☐ Select the File menu.
- ☐ Select Import (or type command-Shift-I).
- ☐ Locate and choose the image(s) you wish to import.
- ☐ Click the Review for Import button.
- ☐ Click Import All New Photos in the upper right corner to confirm your photos.

Now, the file has been uploaded to your Photos library.

You may also import photographs from the Finder by dragging and dropping them onto the Photos icon; Photos will import them.

Keep in mind, though, that Photos does not include original photos in imports by default. It maintains connections to them, allowing you to utilize photos to modify or catalog them without moving them.

This is a sword with two edges: It minimizes the size of the photographs' library, but it might be perplexing if your objective is to organize folders and disks containing numerous photos. To ensure that imported files are copied to your photos library, you must set Photos' options to transfer imported files to the photos library. If you intend to share those imported photographs on other devices, there's a second crucial reason to do so: iCloud Photo Library will only upload objects that have been copied to the photos' library.

Instructions for copying imported files to your Photos library

1. Click the Photos icon while Photos is open.
2. Select Settings...
3. Select the Copy to Photos Library checkbox.

This ensures that only objects that have been copied to the library are uploaded to iCloud Photos.

How to import iPhoto into Photos for macOS

If you're switching from iPhoto to Photos for Mac and you've never had more than one iPhoto library on your Mac, the upgrade method is straightforward: Photos will automatically import all of your iPhoto photographs once you use the program for the first time.

If you need to utilize iPhoto for whatever reason, your old iPhoto library will remain, but updates made to older photographs will not immediately sync with your new Photos library. If you no longer use your old iPhoto library, you may dump it - your photographs are now stored securely in Photos (and if you've enabled iCloud Photo Library, in iCloud as well).

If you are using numerous libraries, photos for Mac is compatible with a maximum of one primary library per Mac: This implies that it is not possible to integrate many old iPhoto or Aperture libraries into a single master library.

Therefore, if you have numerous libraries on your computer, Photos will prompt you to choose which library to import when you first run the application. After selecting the desired library, Photos will prepare and import the photographs.

While holding down the Option key and clicking on Photos, a pop-up menu will display.

In the Choose Library pop-up, select the desired Library to open. Tap the Select Library button.

You may still update your other older libraries to separate Photos libraries; you'll simply have to import each one individually by using the Option key before launching the Photos application.

The only difference between these other Photos libraries is that only one may be synchronized with iCloud Photo Library at a time. Your other files will be isolated locally (or externally, if they are stored on a hard drive) from iCloud's sync service.

Videos

QuickTime Player offers on-screen controls for playing, pausing, fast-forwarding, and rewinding music and video files.

Using the playback controls, you can also play a file on an AirPlay-enabled device, display a video in a picture-in-picture window, share a file, and adjust the playback speed.

Open a file

To open a video or music file with the QuickTime Player application on your Mac, you can:

- ▢ Click the file twice in the Finder.
- ▢ If your films or music files are stored in iCloud Drive, click iCloud Drive in the Finder's sidebar, then double-click the file you wish

to access. See You can store documents on your Mac, iPhone, and iPad using iCloud Drive.

☐ Select a file, then select File > Open File, and click Open.

☐ Before playing a file with an older or third-party media format, QuickTime Player may convert it.

☐ You may also open a file you've recently worked on by selecting File > Open Recent.

Invoke a file

The playback controls that display when the mouse cursor is over the screen allow you to play and control a file. You may fast forward and rewind, as well as adjust the playback speed.

1. Launch the QuickTime Player application on your Mac and load a video or audio file.
2. Place the cursor anywhere on the video to display its playback controls. (Audio file controls are always available.)
3. Use the playback controls to play the video or audio file; you can move the controls out of the way by dragging them.
4. If your Mac has a Touch Bar, you can utilize the Touch Bar to control playback.

You may adjust the video's playing speed using the forward and rewind buttons. Click the forward or backward button until the movie is playing at the appropriate pace to adjust the playback speed. The available playback speeds are 2x, 5x, 10x, 30x, and 60x.

Option-clicking the forward or rewind button, while a video is playing, allows you to alter the playback speed in minor increments (from 1.1x to 2x).

You may also select a playback speed before the video begins to play. Click the Share and Playback Speed option, then select Playback Speed and the desired speed.

If you want the currently playing file to display on top of all other windows, select View > Float on Top so that a checkmark appears next to it. Select it again to disable it.

A video with picture-in-picture will be played.

With picture-in-picture, you may play a movie in a resizable floating window, allowing you to view it while performing other computer operations.

- ⬚ Launch QuickTime Player on your Mac and load a video file.
- ⬚ Place the cursor anywhere on the video to display its playback controls.
- ⬚ Click the picture-in-picture button in the controls for playback.
- ⬚ You may slide the picture-in-picture window to a different screen corner or resize it by dragging any window edge.
- ⬚ Click the full-screen button or the close button to close the window with window within a window.

Play a file in an endless loop.

You may arrange a video or audio file to play constantly, such that it plays from beginning to end and then begins again.

- ⬚ Open the audio or video file that you wish to loop.
- ⬚ Select View > Loop to add a checkbox next to it.

☐ Click the Play button on the controller for playback.

☐ Select the command again to disable continuous play; the checkmark disappears.

Navigate a video using timecode

You may modify the playback controls' display to show the elapsed time, frame count, or timecode (depending on the characteristics of the video).

Some media files display an 8-digit timecode (00-00-00-00) in the playing controls, as opposed to the 4-digit remaining time code. The timecode displays source time information for a given frame or recorded moments, such as the recording time or frame number. You may utilize the timecode to travel to a specific frame in a media file while exploring a project.

☐ Modify the presentation of the playback controls: Select View > Time Display, then select the desired display choice.

⬚   Move to a certain time-coded frame: Select View > Time Display > Go To Timecode, and then input the desired timecode.

Books

If you are an Apple user, the Books application is the best option for reading on your Mac. This is particularly convenient if you also use Books on your iPhone and iPad, as you can resume reading where you left off on your computer.

The Books application on macOS is simple to use, but let's examine how to launch a book and personalize your reading experience.

⬚   Select a book using the navigation on the left. If you connect your iPhone and iPad, you may access a book you've already begun by visiting Reading Now. You may also access all of your books, samples, and PDFs in the Library area. And towards the bottom, you may access one of the My Collections groupings.

⬚   If a book has a cloud icon underneath it, it must be downloaded to your Mac in order to be read. Click the Cloud or the three dots next to it, and then pick Download.

⬚   To open the book, simply double-click on it. The book will open in a separate window that may be customized to enhance the reading experience. Position the pointer at the top of the window to see the toolbar.

⬚   Click the Theme and Appearance icon (aA) on the right to launch a tiny pop-up window.

⬚   You may increase or decrease the font size by clicking the large or tiny A at the top.

- ▢ Choose a color for your theme from white, sepia, gray, or black. If you select a dark color, the typeface will change to a light hue automatically, and vice versa.
- ▢ You are then able to pick a font style. This is ideal for a novel or manual with basic print in a traditional manner.
- ▢ Click the arrow on the right or left, or swipe with your trackpad or Magic Mouse, to turn the pages.
- ▢ As you read, the Books app provides extra tools in the toolbar. There are three icons on the left that display the table of contents, bookmarks, and highlights or notes.
- ▢ On the right of the symbol for the book's theme and look are icons for sharing the book, searching inside it, and bookmarking the current page.
- ▢ To dismiss a book you are currently reading, click the red X in the top left corner of the window. You will then return to the Books window's main screen.

Mac users may access the Kindle app to read books.

The Kindle app is another wonderful program for reading books on a Mac (free in the App Store). This choice is beneficial if you have a Kindle e-reader, utilize the web-based reader, or have the Kindle app on your mobile device. Similar to the Books app, it is possible to sync and continue reading on the Mac.

Step 1: Select a book using the left-hand navigation. In addition to PDFs and collections, you may view all or downloaded books by clicking the corresponding links. Double-click a book to launch it. If required, the book will automatically download.

Step 2: Similar to Apple Books on the Mac, you can personalize your reading experience in the Kindle app by clicking the Aa icon in the toolbar.

- Choose from over a dozen font styles, ranging from basic to formal.
- Size of the font: Use the slider to raise or reduce the font size.
- Choose between Justified and Left-Alignment for the page alignment.
- Select Small, Medium, or Large for the line spacing option.
- Width of the page: Use the slider to adjust the width of the page as it appears in the window.
- Use the slider to modify the display's brightness from dark to light.
- Choose from White, Black, or Sepia for the color mode. The typeface will automatically adjust to a dark or light shade based on the color you select.
- You can pick a single-column, multiple-column, or auto-fit layout option to the right of the appearance icon.

Step 3: To flip the pages, click the right and left Arrows or use your trackpad or Magic Mouse to swipe.

Step 4: As you read, you will see more icons in the toolbar and on the left-hand side.

- On the left side of the toolbar, you may return to the Library, go Back, refresh the page, or Go To a specific location in the book. Mark the current page as a Favorite or click Show Notebook to view highlights or notes.
- On the window's left-hand side are three icons for Table of Contents, Search, and Flashcards.
- To close a book, click Library on the toolbar's left side. Your current reading position is automatically stored.

It is handy to read a book on your Mac during a coffee break, when utilizing reference material, or when accessing a handbook for a project. You may always use both Apple Books and Kindle if you cannot choose!

Music

With the release of macOS Catalina, the Music app for Mac replaced iTunes and consolidated Apple Music and your personal music library into a single area. While the demise of iTunes was somewhat distressing for some, macOS Big Sur has demonstrated that the Music app for Mac will remain.

If you are acquainted with iTunes or the iOS Music app, you will likely find the Music app to be intuitive to use. This is a fast refresher on playing music, organizing your collection, and navigating the Music app for Mac if you are new to the Music app. Thus, your finest Mac may resume playing your favorite music. Here's how to utilize the Mac Music app.

How to play music within the Mac music application

A few taps are all it takes to begin playing music in the Music app; you're off to the races.

- ☐ Launch Music from the Dock or Applications directory.
- ☐ Click the play button that appears while hovering over the desired album or playlist.
- ☐ If you wish to play a certain song, click the album or playlist.
- ☐ Click the play button that appears on the album image or track number when hovering over it in the tracklist.

How to view your music collection in the Mac music app

Your music collection is also integrated directly into the Music app. You may explore your full collection by artist, album, or song, as well as view newly added tracks. Even the sorting strategy of your collection may be altered.

- Launch Music from the Dock or Applications directory.
- Click Recently Added in the sidebar to browse recently added albums and tracks (but not playlists) to your collection.
- Click Artists on the sidebar to peruse your library's collection of musical artists.
- Select View from the menu.
- Hover over Sort Albums By.
- Click Title, Genre, Year, or Rating to filter results.
- Click the Ascending or Descending button.
- To peruse your music library by album, click Albums on the sidebar.
- Select View from the menu.
- Select Display View Options
- Click the drop-down menu adjacent to then: to select Title, Artist, Year, or Rating.
- To view your songs, click on Songs. Many would claim that this is the traditional iTunes perspective, dating back over two decades to the initial release.
- By clicking the Name, Time, Artist, Album, Genre, or other category bars, you may organize your music according to these criteria.

How to add music to the Mac music application

- Importing songs into the Music app is comparable to how it was previously accomplished in iTunes.
- Launch Music from the Dock or Applications directory.
- Select File from the Menu Bar.

- ☐ Click the Import button.
- ☐ Select the desired file or folder to import.
- ☐ Click Open.

How to access song and album information in the Mac music app

You may right-click on any track to modify its details (such as the album, artist, and year) if you wish to personalize your collection.

- ☐ Launch Music from the Dock or Applications directory.
- ☐ Control- or right-click on a song or album.
- ☐ Click Get Info.
- ☐ If you are modifying several songs, click Edit Items.
- ☐ If necessary, modify information under the Details, Artwork, Lyrics, Options, Sorting, and File tabs.
- ☐ When editing is complete, click OK.
- ☐ You can right-click on tracks in Apple Music to view track details, but you cannot alter the information.

2.5 Use iCloud

If you want to get the most out of your Mac, you must use iCloud. Here is how to begin doing that.

iCloud is integral to Apple's ecosystem. When enabled, the service allows the synchronization of data across numerous devices via a secure server.

If you use many Apple products, iCloud is an excellent way to keep your contacts and calendar events up to date.

And even if you drop your Mac down a well, get it stolen by a monkey, or experience some other misfortune, your data will be stored on a server that is retrievable.

iCloud is an essential feature for contemporary Mac users. So let's examine how to configure and utilize iCloud on your Mac.

How to Create an iCloud Account

If you already have an Apple ID, you may sign in to iCloud through System Preferences > Apple ID and follow the on-screen instructions to configure iCloud. If you do not already have an Apple account, though, you may create one at the same spot on your Mac.

Here are the steps to creating an iCloud account:

- ⬚ An Apple ID can be accessed by selecting System Preferences > Apple ID from the Apple menu.

Apple ID   Family Sharing

- ⬚
- ⬚ Tap "Create an Apple ID."
- ⬚ Enter your date of birth, then click Continue.
- ⬚ Enter your name, email, and password, then click Next. If you don't want to use your current email address, you may establish a new one by clicking Get a free iCloud email address.
- ⬚ Follow the on-screen directions to complete the installation.

In most countries, the minimum age to create an Apple ID without parental consent is 13. Age restrictions differ by area; thus, you should contact Apple Support for additional information. If a youngster is too young to establish their own account, you can create one for them via Family Sharing.

After creating an Apple ID and completing the verification process, macOS should immediately sign you into your new iCloud account.

You will eventually get a window asking if you wish to integrate some data, such as contacts and calendars.

To begin synchronizing the listed data, choose Merge. If you want to select things separately, you may click Don't Merge and proceed with the setup once you've successfully logged in.

Find My Mac can also be enabled by clicking Allow when requested.

On your Mac, which iCloud features should you utilize?

After signing in to iCloud, the Apple ID System Preferences will provide a selection of functions that you may enable. If you do not see this list, click iCloud on the sidebar.

The decision on which services to activate boils down to a single question: what information do you wish to sync with iCloud?

If you do not utilize some of the above services, you likely do not need to waste storage space synchronizing them.

However, the majority of services won't consume a great deal of space, so you may wish to enable them nonetheless.

Let's examine each iCloud function so you can determine which ones are worth activating.

Photos

With Photos enabled, iCloud will synchronize your photos and videos across all of your devices with the service enabled. However, media content can consume a considerable amount of space, so you may need to expand your iCloud storage if you have a large number of items.

Once Photos is enabled, you may modify its settings by navigating to Photos > Preferences > iCloud in the Photos app.

iCloud Keychain is ideal for synchronizing your usernames, passwords, and payment information across many devices in a safe manner. Obviously, you should only enable this capability on devices you fully control.

Cloud Storage

Similar to an online hard drive, iCloud Drive may be used to store other crucial things, such as papers. The service is great for backing up items that you cannot afford to lose, especially if you do not do Time Machine backups regularly.

Clicking Options in System Preferences > Apple ID > iCloud enables you to select which extra files are saved to iCloud Drive. Access iCloud Drive using the Finder's sidebar to manually upload files to the server.

iCloud Mail

By activating iCloud Mail, your iCloud email address is added to the Mac Mail application. Additional settings, including blacklisted senders, signatures, and rules, will sync to the server if iCloud Mail is also chosen in your iCloud Drive preferences.

Notes, Contacts, Calendars, and Reminders

If you own numerous Apple devices, synchronizing your contacts, calendars, reminders, and notes across all of them is quite beneficial. In addition, if something were to happen to your Mac, all of this vital information would still be accessible on the server.

Safari

When Safari for iCloud is enabled, bookmarks, reading lists, and active tabs may be synchronized across several devices. This feature is excellent for facilitating a smooth experience and increasing productivity.

Locate My Mac

Find My Mac enables you to remotely locate, lock, and wipe your Mac. In most situations, there is no valid reason to disable this function. If your Mac gets gone, you will at least have a chance of locating it or stopping a thief from utilizing it.

News Enabling News in iCloud synchronizes some data to the server, including channels, saved stories, and reading history. This function is particularly useful if you read the news on numerous devices.

Enabling iCloud Stocks synchronizes your watch list across many devices.

Home

When iCloud Home is enabled, information about your HomeKit accessories is synchronized to the server for usage on other devices.

Siri

Siri's interaction with you alters its behavior based on your usage. By syncing it to iCloud, you may access your trained and customized version of Apple's artificial intelligence assistant on numerous devices.

Cover My Email and Personal Relay

You may utilize the Hide My Email and Private Relay capabilities if you have an iCloud+ membership, which is essentially a paid iCloud upgrade.

Hide My Email enables you to create a fake email address to use online so that you do not have to reveal your actual information. Using this feature is an excellent method for avoiding spam. Private Relay is a security technology that enables private online browsing. When activated, the service conceals your IP address and other personal data from prying eyes.

Enhancing Your iCloud Storage

If you run out of iCloud storage, you may always purchase extra space. Apple provides a variety of iCloud pricing schemes. Here's how to pgrade your Mac's iCloud storage:

- ⏴ Select System Preferences > Apple ID from the menu.
- ⏴ Select iCloud from the navigation bar.
- ⏴ Click Manage in the window's footer.
- ⏴ Click Add Storage.
- ⏴ Select a new storage plan, then click Next to finish the update.
- ⏴ iCloud is a requirement for modern Mac users.
- ⏴ If you're a modern Mac user, iCloud is an indispensable and virtually essential utility. Syncing vital information facilitates access from many devices and prevents data loss.

Some iCloud features are more intriguing than others, but the vast majority of users will discover at least one that simplifies their life.

2.6 Control Center

The 'Control Center' symbol is located in the upper-right corner of the menu bar. Select the symbol to access the functionality. You will find shortcuts to settings such as 'Wi-Fi', 'Bluetooth', 'AirDrop', 'Do Not Disturb', 'Keyboard Brightness', and 'Screen Mirroring' on 'Control Center'. Click the shortcut to access its configuration. For instance, choosing the 'Wi-Fi' shortcut displays a list of accessible networks from which you may choose.

There are also volume and display brightness controls. Additionally, you may play, stop, and skip items within the "Music" app.

You can drag any shortcut from the 'Control Center' onto the menu bar to set it there. To remove an item from the menu bar, hold down the command key and drag the item out of the bar.

Customizing Mac Control Panel

In macOS Big Sur, Apple offers minimal customization options for the 'Control Center'. You may alter the settings by selecting "Apple" from the menu bar's upper-left corner. Choose System Preferences > Dock & Menu Bar from the menu.

The Control Center item shortcuts are located in the Control Center section. These cannot be deleted from the "Control Center," but their visibility on the menu bar can be modified.

Below the Other Modules section are other Control Center shortcuts that can be added. To add an item, pick it and then tick the 'Show in Control Center' box. Check the 'Show in Menu Bar' checkbox to include the item there as well.

Lastly, beneath the Menu Bar Only section are the keyboard shortcuts that are exclusive to the menu bar. You may add or remove them as necessary.

2.7 Notifications & Widget

Since OS X 10.4 (Tiger) in 2005, Apple's macOS has enabled widgets as a part of the operating system. They belonged to the Dashboard application at the time. These mini-applications were shown on a separate desktop. Stickies, weather, and a calculator were among the built-in widgets.

However, in 2019, macOS Catalina eliminated the Dashboard and transferred widgets to the Notification Center.

What Exactly Are Widgets?

Widgets are tiny, self-contained applications that offer limited information and functionality.

In macOS Big Sur, Apple arranged widgets in the Notification Center as a two-column grid beneath any notifications. Each widget may be either tiny, medium, or huge.

You may see widgets by accessing the Notification Center at any moment. If you utilize widgets frequently, it is beneficial to add a keyboard shortcut to this activity.

How to Insert, Delete, and Relocate Apple Widgets

When the Notification Center is active (to Open Notification Centre: Click the date and time in the menu bar, or swipe left with two fingers from the right edge of the trackpad.), an Edit Widgets button appears at the very bottom. This link will launch the editing overlay. This toggles between the view and edit modes. Your existing widget list stays on the right, while a list of available widgets appears on the left.

To add a widget, you may drag it from the available list and place it in the correct location on the Notification Center overlay. Clicking the green plus (+) symbol in the upper-left corner of a widget moves it to the end of the list.

When installing a widget, if many sizes are available, you can select one. MacOS picks the smallest size by default. To use a different size, click the S, M, or L icons underneath the widget prior to its addition.

In edit mode, a widget can be removed by clicking the minus sign (-) in the upper-left corner. In either mode, you can also delete a widget by controlling-clicking and selecting Remove Widget.

Widgets may be moved in either standard view mode or edit mode. Simply relocate a widget by dragging and dropping it.

How to Modify Particular Widgets

Some widgets allow for modification. Those that do will enlarge somewhat when you hover over them while in edit mode. In addition, they will have an Edit Widget label towards the bottom. This button allows you to modify a widget.

Changing the city of the clock widget or choosing a different topic for the news widget are instances of customization.

Which Widgets Can Be Installed on a Mac?

Built-in Widgets macOS allows many widgets for its native applications. The following applications include one or two widgets by default:

- Calendar\sClock\sNews\sNotes
- Photos\sPodcasts\sReminders
- Screen Time Securities
- Widgets From Third-Party Weather Applications
- Many app developers have opted to integrate their own Notification Center widgets, which is permitted. As the new location for widgets on macOS becomes more established, more applications should add support.

Fantastical is a calendar application with a variety of widgets for displaying your events in different ways. They range from a basic glimpse of the current date to widgets presenting a list of upcoming events, a tiny calendar, and the current weather.

Bear, the app for taking notes, provides widgets for displaying a single note and recent notes for a search keyword.

AirBuddy 2 is an application for monitoring battery conditions. It utilizes widgets effectively to display the power levels of your numerous Bluetooth devices.

Utilize Widgets to Quickly Access Vital Information

As part of the Notification Center, Apple makes widgets more accessible than ever before, allowing you to incorporate them into your daily routine. Widgets enable instantaneous access to the most important information on your Mac.

Widgets function optimally in tiny amounts. If you are experiencing information overload, consider reviewing our recommendations on how to maintain concentration.

2.8 Use Apple Pay

Using Apple Pay on your Mac mini, you may make purchases on websites in a simple, safe, and confidential manner. Apple does not keep or disclose your Apple Card or other credit or debit card information with merchants using Apple Pay. When shopping online with Safari, look for Apple Pay as a payment option. Use your Magic Keyboard with Touch ID, iPhone, or Apple Watch to confirm your transaction.

Apple Pay and Apple Card are not accessible in all areas or countries. To learn more about Apple Pay, visit Apple Pay. See the Apple Support page Apple Pay Participating Banks for information on current card issuers. Apple Card information may be found at Apple Card Support.

Configure Apple Pay. If you have already set up credit or debit cards on your iPhone or Apple Watch, no additional setup is necessary. You may configure your debit and credit cards under the Wallet & Apple Pay section of System Preferences if you haven't already. Ensure that your iPhone and Apple Watch are logged in with the same Apple ID as your Mac mini.

Purchase items with your iPhone or Apple Watch. Click the Apple Pay button on the website, then use Face ID, Touch ID, or the passcode on your iPhone to authenticate the payment, or double-click the side button on your unlocked Apple Watch. You must be signed in to an Apple Pay-enabled iPhone or Apple Watch with the same Apple ID used on your Mac mini.

You can manage your Apple Card and add or remove payment cards under the Wallet & Apple Pay section of System Preferences.

Chapter 3: Using the Internet

3.1 Using Safari and other browsers

Apple has recently added new capabilities to its Safari browser, making the primary Mac application for online exploration speedier and more robust. However, if you desire a change, there are many different browsers available, like Microsoft Edge, Chrome, Firefox, Brave, and many others. This article compiles the finest alternatives to Safari and examines their features.

You may also be interested in learning about DuckDuckGo, which has been published as a browser but is only available to beta testers at this time. We will do an evaluation of the new web browser as soon as we can get our hands on it. In the meantime, read further here: The beta version of DuckDuckGo's privacy-focused Mac browser has been released.

Safari

Apple's Safari browser has been around for a long time, and it has evolved to the point that it is now a pretty strong option for the vast majority of users. It has bookmarks, tabbed browsing, a password manager, private browsing settings, a dark mode, a read later list, and a Shared with You area on the home page that shows links provided to you via Messages.

The reading mode is still one of Safari's best-kept secrets since it transforms every web page into a sleek, distraction-free article.

With the release of macOS Monterey and version 15, Apple introduced Tab Groups, a useful new feature that allows you to group certain tabs by a category of your choice, so you don't have to hunt for them among your other active tabs. This is especially helpful if you are organizing a vacation, or event, or investigating a different hobby. Group Tabs synchronize with Safari on your iPhone, iPad, and other Macs.

Integral to Apple's offering is Intelligent Tracking Protection, which prevents marketers from tracking your activity. This is accompanied by anti-fingerprinting settings that prohibit websites from analyzing your hardware and software setup to determine your online identity, as well as security measures that block potentially malware-infected websites.

Apple Pay is also fully integrated, making it simple to purchase products online using the Touch ID sensor on Macs with Touch Bars or your iPhone. See How to Use Apple Pay on a Mac for further information.

In its current state, Safari is better than ever, and that's before you investigate the various extensions that can expand its powers. The best browser for your Mac is most likely already installed.

Chrome

Chrome remains, by a wide margin, the most popular desktop browser in the world, but this includes Windows users. Chrome is a great tool with a vast ecosystem of plug-ins and extensions, ranging from privacy monitors to ones that correct your grammar, so it's easy to understand why it's so popular.

However, Chrome handles multiple tabs fairly well. Nevertheless, leaving a large number of tabs open at once might result in Chrome hogging RAM. Nonetheless, this is true of most browsers. In operation, it is quick. Pages are produced rapidly and there is a global zoom setting, which might be useful if you find text on current websites to be too tiny.

As expected, Chrome integrates seamlessly with Google's web apps, such as Drive, Docs, Calendar, Photos, and Translate, allowing users to activate them from an app tray in the menu bar. You may also use accessible browser extensions, such as Google Keep, to generate reminders straight from the browser.

Chrome's extensions are what distinguish it from other browsers, and there are over 150,000 to pick from. You may use password managers like Dashlane, the coupon checker Honey, Grammarly, and so much more to improve your writing. To view our favorite Chrome extensions, visit Best Chrome Extensions. Chrome's password storage is safe, and it may save your payment information so that it's easier to make online payments, although Apple Pay is not supported.

Google employs stringent security measures to prevent you from accessing sites containing malware and separates each tab to prevent cross-contamination should you stumble onto something malicious. Obviously, this is Google we're talking about, so when you use Chrome, you'll be providing the firm with your data, including your internet habits, so make sure you're comfortable with that before you start.

Firefox

Firefox is another veteran that has just received a much-needed polish. There was once a time when this was one of the leading browsers, but time has not been kind to Mozilla's invention, and Google Chrome in particular has been luring users away. This is unfortunate, given the current version of

Firefox is sleek, intelligent, and a great alternative to its more prominent competitors.

Mozilla takes privacy seriously and provides a variety of safety features to keep you secure online. Tracking Protection prevents websites from tracking your web activity and gathering data that can be used to display advertisements. There is also ad and script blocking, which accelerates the loading of online pages. There is also a plugin that sandboxes Facebook so that it cannot track your web habits. Regardless of the modifications behind the hood, our experience with the app shows that it is quick and dependable. Firefox has always been a customizable browser, so make sure to check out the available themes and extensions that can be used to beautify the browser's menu bar or add other functions. By dragging icons onto the menu bar, you may perform a variety of actions, such as emailing links, storing the page to Firefox's Pocket program for later reading, or sending pages directly to your mobile device.

There may not be as many extensions for Firefox as there are for Chrome, but there are many helpful add-ons that allow you to customize Firefox to your liking. Mozilla provides other tools, such as Relay (similar to iCloud Private Relay), which generates email aliases for use while signing up for online services or providing to individuals to whom you do not wish to reveal your actual email address. A VPN that can conceal your location, together with a monitor that checks for password breaches that may have compromised any of your accounts. Firefox may not be as powerful as it once was, but it still has plenty of life.

Opera

Opera is based on the same foundations as Chrome, which gives it a familiar feel in terms of

performance and functionality. This does not imply that it is only a clone with a different logo, though, since the app's design and tools make it a thoroughly contemporary web browser.

The first is a column on the screen's left with shortcuts to different choices. All of Facebook Messenger, WhatsApp, Telegram, and Instagram can be accessed while browsing the web. There is also the option to add a Twitter account, which is really beneficial if you want to avoid constantly picking up your phone.

My Flow is a feature exclusive to Opera that allows users to transmit web pages straight to their iPhone. Three dots at the bottom of the column launch the settings menu. In this part, you may add or delete many other icons that go to your bookmarks, a news section that compiles the latest headlines from your favorite publications, and a speed dial for frequently visited sites.

In addition to a built-in ad blocker and a free VPN, Opera's privacy features make browsing more convenient. Even though the number of server locations is restricted, the second option is superior for securing public WiFi connections.

Due to Chrome's background, an abundance of extensions are available, as are themes for customizing the browser's appearance. Workspaces, which are effectively the same as Group Tabs in Safari, are now also available. Here, you add new Workspaces (naming them and selecting an appropriate icon) and then opening several tabs within each one. This allows you to rapidly browse between related websites, streamlining your experience and preventing you from having a million tabs open simultaneously.

Opera provides several advantages if you seek a browser that not only protects your online privacy but also lowers the need for other applications on your machine.

3.2 Navigate the Internet

Menu bar

Using the mouse, you may access the menu bar positioned at the very top of the screen. When you hold down the mouse button over an item in the main menu, a submenu with more options is "drawn down." Actions that cannot be carried out are shown in gray or lighter shades of black. The submenus give keyboard shortcuts for numerous frequent activities, allowing you to execute them more quickly than with the mouse.

Address Field

In addition to being situated at the top of the browser window, the address bar features Web navigation buttons and a field for entering the URL of any website or page you wish to visit. The following buttons are featured in Safari's address bar by default:

Command Function

- Back Returns the user to the previous page.
- Forward Proceeds to the following page
- Reload Reloads and shows the current page.
- Add Bookmark Saves the current page's address so you may return to it later.
- You may simply alter the address bar's buttons by selecting View, Customize Address Bar...

A window with buttons that may be dragged to the address bar will appear.

For instance, you may add a home button that, when clicked, will send you immediately to the website you have designated as your home page, or a stop button that will prevent a page from fully loading. You may also drag the default set displayed at the bottom of the window to restore the default setting of the address bar.

The address bar also contains a search box where you can do a Google search for pages and websites containing your search parameters. Click the tiny arrow pointing downwards next to To view a list of past searches, click the magnifying glass symbol in the search field. You will then be presented with a list of your recent searches. If you like, you will find the option to clear recent searches at the bottom of the list.

Status bar

The browser's status bar is situated at the very bottom of the window. When hovering over a link on a web page, the status bar displays the complete URL. Select View, Hide Status Bar if you do not wish to view the status bar.

Scroll bar

The scroll bar is the vertical bar on the right-hand side of the browser window. By placing the mouse cursor on the slider control and depressing the mouse button, you may scroll up and down a web page.

If you have installed the Mac version of Mozilla Firefox, your browser window will have a layout very similar to that described above.

To add additional buttons to the toolbar (which is not referred to as the address bar in Firefox), click View, Toolbars, and Customize.

As with Safari, you may drag the buttons you wish to add to the toolbar, or you can click the Restore Default Set button to restore the toolbar to its default configuration.

Firefox for the Mac differs from Safari in that it supports many search engines for doing web searches. It is not exclusive to Google alone.

To view a list of available search engines, click the little arrow pointing downwards next to the magnifying glass symbol in the search field.

This displays a list of available search engines.

You may also pick Add Engine to access a page on the Mozilla website where you can add more search engines.

3.3 Downloading Files

Depending on the sort of thing you wish to store, you may save Safari content to your Mac in a variety of ways. While some internet content cannot be downloaded, files, photos, software, and apps frequently include a dedicated download button. Otherwise, Control-click or double-tap an item to download or save it.

It is advisable not to download software or applications from unreliable sources.

Location of Safari Downloads on a Mac

Downloaded goods from Safari have automatically been placed in your Downloads folder unless you've specified otherwise. To locate this file, use Finder and choose Downloads from the sidebar or press Cmd + Option + L.

If desired, you can alter the location where downloaded files are saved:

- Navigate to Safari > Options.
- Select the Basics tab. Go to the File download location, then select from the menu that appears. If you want additional control over each download, choose to Ask for each download.
- If you wish to choose a specific destination, click Other and choose the folder you want.
- Use Safari's Downloads Button
- You can quickly access your downloads in Safari by clicking the Downloads button, a circle with a downward-pointing arrow, located in the upper-right corner of the Safari window. This will only show if you have recently downloaded an item.

Launch the Downloads Stack in the Dock.

The Dock is another option to rapidly access your downloaded files. Recent downloads are typically stacked on the right side of the dock. You may preview its contents by hovering over it or clicking to enlarge it.

Using Finder, open the Downloads folder.

As previously said, you may also locate Safari downloads using Finder. This is a useful tool for locating stuff on our Mac. Simply click the magnifying glass icon on your menu bar and enter "downloads," or select Finder in your dock to launch the Finder window.

Typically, the Downloads folder may be found on the sidebar, under Favorites.

How to Manage Downloads in Safari

Safari provides many options for managing your ongoing and completed downloads. To perform these operations, launch Safari's Downloads menu. Here are your options:

- Pause Downloads: To pause a download, click the stop button next to the file's name, and then click the restart button to resume the download.
- Find a Downloaded Item: If your Mac is crowded and you cannot locate a downloaded file, click the magnifying glass next to the file's name to open it in Finder.
- To remove a single downloaded item from the list, Control-click the item and select Remove from List. Clicking Clear in the upper-right corner of the pop-up will also erase all recently downloaded goods.

By default, Safari deletes all downloaded files after one day. If you wish to modify this:

- Select "Safari" > "Options."
- Select General, then Remove things from the download list. Choose between After one day, When Safari exits, Upon successful download, and Manually.
- Manage Downloads in Safari

There is a great deal of content that can be downloaded from the Internet, and understanding how to do so is typically half the battle. Then, you can use the suggestions in this article to locate and manage your Safari downloads with ease, including adjusting your download options to have greater control over where your files are saved and when they are erased.

3.5 Best Websites for Seniors

While some members of the younger generation believe that older folks and the Internet do not mix, an increasing number of retirees have been comfortable navigating the Internet for at least two decades.

In fact, the majority of those who claim to have invented the Internet (including Al Gore) are of retirement age or older.

And while millions of people use the Internet every day to listen to the newest music, update their social statuses, and for some reason take pictures of the food they're about to eat, there are hundreds upon hundreds of useful websites designed specifically for senior citizens that contain information that can make your life easier, save you money, maximize the benefits you're entitled to, and help you plan for the future.

Here are some of the top online resources for elderly citizens in a variety of fields.

AARP (aarp.org) is the go-to site for anything related to older folks, including money guidance, queries about health benefits, and where to discover savings across the board, regardless of whether you are a member or not. Even better, the website provides advice to everyone who has reached the age of 50 and is beginning to see the end of the road in their journey towards retirement.

The majority of us visit three government websites throughout our lifetimes: the Internal Revenue Service, Medicaid, and the Post Office. Not exactly an enticing recommendation for wanting to see something else administered by the United States government, right?

However, the **Administration on Aging (AOA)** website is well-organized and has a wealth of important information, notably on health and nutrition, as well as the most recent data on aging, free news stories, and an eNewsletter.

ThirdAge (thirdage.com): It seems a little like a video game title, but it's actually a pun on your childhood being your first age, your working years being your second age, and the third age being "healthy living for now and beyond." The site features an excellent Health A-Z encyclopedia that is simply accessible and searchable, as well as articles and blogs on aging well, lifestyle, relationships, and everything else under the sun for today's seniors, as well as the option to attend online classes.

SeniorNet (seniornet.org) was founded in 1986 to give older persons the chance to learn about and utilize computer technology. This not only enables you to keep up with technology as it swiftly alters the way we interact, pay our bills, save our records, etc., but it may also provide you an advantage in maintaining your employment for as long as you choose.

National Senior Persons Law Center (nsclc.org): Among the most difficult aspects of aging is the fact that senior citizens are the primary target of con artists in the United States. Complex systems such as Medicare, wills, estates, retirement homes, and financial investments can be baffling to the elderly, and there are others who prey on the elderly for their own financial benefit, given that our mental faculties tend to deteriorate with age. The National Senior Citizens Law Center (NSCLC) campaigns for senior rights on a broad scale, providing assistance, guidance, and support for a variety of needs.

Buzz 50 (buzz50.com) is an exclusive social network for seniors. Yes! Buzz 50 is a website oriented for adults over the age of 50, particularly recently-retired baby boomers. It offers both discussion forums and chat rooms for seniors to engage with peers not just in the United States but also internationally. Create a profile page and network!

Elder Treks (eldertreks.com): No, it's not supper with William Shatner or tea with Patrick Stewart. Elder Treks enables seniors to organize once-in-a-lifetime journeys that likely wouldn't have been possible during their younger years when job and children responsibilities were of paramount importance. There are both domestic and international destinations, such as Easter Island, the Galapagos Islands, Machu Picchu, Egypt, and Kenya. Activity levels and duration of stay are variable, ranging from a weekend to a month. Obviously, the price tag is a bit steep, but who needs to leave an estate when you can spend 14 days en route to the North Pole aboard the world's largest icebreaker?

Chapter 4: Essential and Popular Apps

4.1 AppStore and Installing Apps

An app store (application shop) is an online marketplace for the acquisition and download of software applications.

All of the main mobile operating system providers, including Apple, Google, BlackBerry, and Microsoft, operate their own app shops, giving them control over the applications accessible for their own platforms. There are also a number of third-party software shops, such as the Amazon Appstore for Android and Cydia for jailbroken Apple iOS devices.

With the emergence of smartphones and tablets, the app store concept gained popularity, but it has now spread to Web browsers and desktop operating systems. Each of the browsers, Mozilla Firefox and Google Chrome, has its own store where users may install Web-based applications. Desktop programs for Mac OS X and Windows 8 are also accessible via app stores.

A related notion is the corporate app store, a portal managed by IT that makes authorized business applications accessible to end users.

Installing applications from the Mac App Store

The Mac App Store is one of the greatest methods for acquiring and installing applications on a Mac. It has benefits and negatives, but the greatest grade is for its usability.

Choose App Store from the Apple menu to launch the Mac App Store. When logged in with an Apple ID, you may download apps: tap Get and then install the app for a free app or one with in-app purchases, or tap the pricing label for a paid app. If there are in-app purchases, they are listed next to the Get button. You must verify payment by entering your Apple

ID and password.

Apple examines each Mac App Store application (and update) before its distribution, thereby limiting the possibility of issues.

The Software Store is also an excellent method for centralizing app updates. In System Preferences > Software Update, you may select to automatically install App Store updates.

How to install Mac applications obtained from external places

Apple sets restrictions on developers, which means that some cannot – or choose not to – publish their applications on the Mac App Store. The reasons vary, ranging from a lack of Deep system access for utilities to software developers who want the option to send updates without waiting for a Mac App Store review.

If you choose to download program installers over the Internet, you should only do so from trustworthy sources. Download apps from developer websites (such as Intego's) rather than app listing websites.

Unless you've altered your browser's settings, downloaded installers will be stored in /Downloads and come in a number of formats:

- DMG files are disk images that are mountable. Double-clicking a DMG file opens the Finder window. DMGs may contain an installer that must be launched before on-screen instructions can be followed. The majority, however, only include a copy of the software.
- Do not launch the application from within the DMG file; instead, drag it to the Applications folder. A folder shortcut might be given to facilitate this. Unmount the DMG after you're finished by clicking the eject icon next to its name in the Finder sidebar or by Ctrl-clicking within the DMG's window and selecting Eject.
- ZIP files (and very rarely RAR files) are archives that typically contain a single application. Repeatedly, drag the application to the Applications folder before launching it. This helps keep

things organized, but certain applications cannot operate unless they are in this folder. (Some will offer to relocate themselves if they are opened in the incorrect area.)

- PKG files are installation packages containing installation-directing scripts and the files to be installed.
- These are often used for applications and utilities that require extra components, system services, and/or files to be deployed elsewhere on your computer and guide you through a multi-step installation procedure. (This is automatic; you only need to click a few times to allow the PKG to perform its function.)

You can remove the DMG, ZIP, or PKG files after installing your software, but if the apps are huge and your bandwidth is restricted, you may want to save them in case you need to reinstall the apps or install them on another Mac.

How to install Mac applications from unofficial app stores

There are various independent alternatives to the Mac App Store. They are often specialized in nature and include a core program that, when launched, allows you to manage which service items are installed on your Mac. Steam is the most popular game shop. It expects you would start buying games from within its app as opposed to /Applications, while it is possible to build desktop shortcuts that may be moved later.

Setapp is a more Mac-like version of a third-party app store. Access to dozens of hand-picked applications is provided for a monthly charge, similar to Netflix. The location of installed applications is /Applications/Setapp. Use Setapp's UI for further administration rather than manually tampering with it.

Clear cautions while installing applications

Upon app installation and activation, your Mac may display security alerts.

For instance, if you download an application from the Internet, your Mac will request confirmation before allowing you to use it for the first time. (This is based on the assumption that the Security & Privacy pane of System Preferences is configured to permit applications downloaded from known developers. That is the default; you may change it by clicking the lock, entering your administrator password, and selecting the appropriate radio box.)

Apps may also seek access to your downloads folder, camera, microphone, and other components the first time they are launched.

In certain situations, such as authorizing access to your Downloads folder, you need only click OK on a dialog box. In others, though, such as the above example, you must visit System Preferences to expressly allow permission. These options are stored in System Preferences > Privacy, where there is a whole column for granting or denying access to applications. To grant permission, you must click the lock icon, enter your password, and then tick the corresponding boxes.

There is an option in the General section of System Preferences to permit apps downloaded from the App Store or from the App Store and specified developers. These latter developers have Apple accounts and sign their programs with an Apple-issued certificate to verify their origin.

However, there are situations when you may wish to launch programs from unknown developers. Select the application in the Finder, then right-click or Control-click and choose Open.

If you attempt to open an application from an unknown developer by double-clicking, you may alternatively launch it by navigating to System Preferences > General and hitting the Open Anyway button towards the bottom of the window. This button will launch the application. The button is displayed for approximately one hour after app activation.

After the first time you run an application, you will no longer need to do this; your Mac will remember your preferences.

4.2 Launching an Application on Mac

This chapter describes how to start programs from the Dock, Recent Items, and Spotlight in macOS.

Out of the Dock

The lengthy strip of icons at the bottom of Mac's display is known as the Dock. Clicking on applications in the Dock is the most common way to start them. The Dock also displays the state of running programs, such as whether they are active or require your attention. Dock icons can also display application-specific information, such as the number of unread email messages in Apple Mail, memory resource use graphs (Activity Monitor), or the current date (Calendar).

Apple populates the Dock by default with a few programs. Finder, Mail, Safari (the default web browser), Contacts, Calendar, Photos, and System Preferences are classic examples.

A program may be added to the Dock by dragging its icon from the Finder onto the Dock. The adjacent Dock icons will shift out of the way to create space. Once an application icon appears in the Dock, the program may be launched by clicking on the icon.

Similarly, an app may be removed from the Dock by dragging its icon from the Dock to the Desktop, where it will vanish in a cloud of smoke.

Removing an application from the dock does not remove it.

To remove an application from the dock, Control-click or right-click the application's icon. From the menu that appears, choose Options > Remove from Dock.

From the List of Recent Items

Select Recent Items from the Apple menu (the Apple symbol in the upper-left corner of the screen). Then, all recently utilized apps, documents, and servers will be shown. Choose the item from the list that you wish to access.

This is not a list of often used products, but of recently used ones, a distinction that is minor but significant.

The Windows Start Menu is comparable to the program launcher seen on iOS devices such as the iPhone and iPad. Clicking the Launchpad icon in the Dock (usually the second icon from the left, unless you've customized the Dock) reveals a layer with huge icons for all the programs installed on your Mac. You may move them around, organize them in folders, and rearrange them in any way you see fit. When an application icon is clicked, the corresponding program is launched.

Not able to locate Launchpad in the Dock? Simply drag it from the Applications folder to the desktop.

In the Applications Directory

The quickest and easiest approach to running an application is to open the Applications folder and click on the desired application. To locate it, launch the Finder from the Dock (it's the first icon on the left).

Clicking on a vacant area of the desktop is another method for launching the Finder.

Choose Applications from the Finder's Go menu, followed by the app you wish to launch.

Using Spotlight on macOS allows you to search for an application by name and run it using Spotlight, an integrated search system available from different locations.

Spotlight is most easily accessible via the menu bar, which runs along the top of your screen. When the magnifying glass symbol is clicked, the Spotlight search box will appear. Enter the full or partial name of the program you wish to locate, and Spotlight will display the results as you type. Double-click a program from the resultant drop-down menu to launch it.

How to Maintain an App Icon on the Dock

macOS will add the application's icon to the Dock if you run it from a location other than the Dock, such as the Applications folder or the Recent Items list. This is just temporary, since the icon will be removed from the Dock when the application is closed.

Control-click or right-click the application's icon in the Dock while the application is running to keep it there. From the menu that appears, choose Options > Keep on Dock.

4.3 Closing and Uninstalling an Application on Mac

Depending on the application, removing it from macOS is as simple as dragging the. The app bundle is placed in the "Bin" However, this does not completely delete the application. If any preference files are left behind,

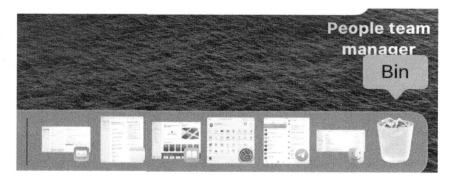

Permanently removing a program is the recommended course of action if

you are attempting to eliminate a corrupt or outdated component. If you want to clear up space on your Mac's hard disk, you also need to do a thorough uninstall. Even when reinstalling software to update a serial number, it is often necessary to first uninstall the previous program.

Okay, this approach is not for the slothful, as it needs some effort. Some strong applications have a propensity to trash your macOS with files in many "/Library/" directories. For this stage, you must be familiar with any names that might be related to the app or applications that will be deleted.

To delete programs from your Mac without leaving traces, you must scan the aforementioned directories for files related to the applications. Take the time to browse through each folder for the application's name and developer. Again, this method is NOT for the slothful.

Obviously, you must know how to access your "Library" folder in order to do this action (ever since the release of macOS X 10.6, it has been hidden, but you should have no trouble unhiding it if you follow the next steps).

1. Open your "Finder." (Cmd+space)

2. Click "Go" when the drop-down option displays.

3. Depress and maintain the Option/Alt key.

4. You will find the "Library" option in the drop-down menu between "Computer" and "Home." Click "Library" to access the directory.

5. Examine the presented list of directories to locate those related to the apps to be removed.

6. After that, use "Finder" to access the "Application Support" folders. Then, look for the directories that hold the data of the uninstalled applications.

There is something more worth mentioning. Additionally, you can discover leftover files in this directory: /Documents/. The majority of software migrated from Windows preserves files in this subdirectory. The same holds true for games ported from Windows to macOS.

Windows programs always save user files in the "Documents" folder. Therefore, when Windows apps are ported to Mac, this behavior is carried over as well.

Lastly, there are hidden directories. By pressing "Command" + "Shift" + ".", you can quickly discover hidden folders in your home directory and determine if they contain any leftover files. Delete any files from the home directory.

How to Close or Force Quit Mac Applications

Force-quitting an application on a Mac may be required for a variety of reasons, the most common being frozen applications. Sometimes you must use sheer force to shut and restart these applications in order to restore their functionality.

Apple is well aware of this, which is why it has provided a variety of solutions for closing recalcitrant applications. You may utilize keyboard shortcuts, third-party applications, and more. One strategy will undoubtedly appeal to you more than the others, but they are all as effective. First on the list is the quickest approach.

Option 1: Macintosh Shortcut

This procedure is very simple and quick. You can force close many applications in a couple of seconds using only your keyboard.

1. Press "Option" + "Command" + "Esc (Escape)".

2. Select the problematic application in the "Force Quit" window that displays.

3. Click the "Force Quit" button.

Option 2: Apple Menu

Using the "Apple Menu" is a more usual way to exit all applications on a Mac. It is just as effective as the shortcut, if not slightly more user-friendly.

1. Open up your "Finder".

2. Go to the menu bar at the top of the page.

3. Click the "Apple" icon placed in the bar's upper-left corner.

4. Select "Force Quit..." from the option that displays.

5. A list of your apps will appear in a new window titled "Force Quit Applications." Select the stalled program and select "Force Quit." That is all. The objective has been attained.

Option 3: Activity Monitor

Windows offers "Task Manager," and Apple has a comparable application. The name of this feature is "Activity Monitor." You may use it to monitor your programs, the performance of your Mac, services, and processes. You can even accomplish much more than this. However, accessing and terminating your programs is a breeze.

1. To display the menu, press "Command" + "Space" on your keyboard. You may also click "Spotlight" in the upper-right corner of your Mac's display.

2. In the "Spotlight Search" field, enter "Activity Monitor."

3. Click "Enter" when you see "Activity Monitor" highlighted.

4. Proceed through the "Activity Monitor" processes list while choosing the frozen applications. The left-hand corner will display "Forcing a process to exit." Click here. All done.

4.4 Mostly used Apps

The finest Mac apps let you get more out of your Mac by expanding on its capabilities and shoring up shortcomings. They make it easier and more enjoyable to use your Mac, boosting your productivity and helping you get more out of your device.

With that in mind, we've put together this list of our top programs to install on a new Mac. Whether you just purchased a sleek new 24-inch Apple iMac 2021 or are looking for some new tools to complement your dependable MacBook Air 2020 (which is still one of the best MacBooks available), these applications will help you get the most from your Mac.

Many of these apps are freely available on the Mac App Store, which you can access by clicking the App Store icon on your Mac's dock (if you can't find it, you can also open the Apple menu in the top-left corner and launch the App Store from there). Because the App Store has hundreds of programs of varying quality, we relied on our own hands-on expertise and user evaluations to compile this list of the finest Mac apps available.

Best Mac productivity apps

Bear

Bear - Markdown Notes 4+
Create, Tag, Export, Encrypt
Shiny Frog Ltd.

★ ★ ★ ★ ★ 4.7 • 3.3K Ratings

Free · Offers In-App Purchases

Bear is a free note-taking app that's versatile, encrypted, and easy to use. While Apple continues to make significant improvements to its own free Notes app, Bear performs many of Notes' functions more efficiently and with a greater emphasis on your privacy. The free version of Bear lets you write notes and to-dos in portable Markdown, organize notes with nested tags, pull assets (like images or text) from web pages into your notes, and even draw or dictate notes using a stylus (for drawing) or Apple Watch (for dictation). If you subscribe to the upgraded Bear Pro version ($14.99/year) you get even more useful features, like the ability to sync notes between devices, encrypt individual notes with a password, or lock the Bear app with Face/Touch ID.

Fantastical

Calendar by Fantastical [4+]
Reminders & Todo List
Flexibits Inc.
★ ★ ★ ★ ★
Free · Offers In-App Purchases

Sure, your Mac already has a built-in calendar, but Fantastical does it better. This award-winning app has long been a favorite of ours. The free edition of Fantastical includes a beautiful, easy-to-use calendar that makes it easy to manage your chores and see what's coming up with a quick glance. If you're willing to pay a monthly fee, you can subscribe to the upgraded version that offers more useful features, including cross-platform Fantastical access and syncing across Mac, iPhone, iPad, and Apple Watch.

Spark

Spark Mail – Smart Email Inbox [4+]
Mailbox organizer & calendar
Readdle Technologies Limited
★ ★ ★ ★ ★
Free · Offers In-App Purchases

You can do better than the default Mail app on macOS, and Spark is one of the best alternatives. This free email client offers a number of handy features the competition doesn't, including a suite of tools that make it easy for multiple people to manage an inbox by doing things like assigning emails to each other or composing emails collaboratively in real-time. It also offers excellent tools for organizing your inbox, scheduling emails, and finding exactly the message you're looking for using a natural language search engine. You can also find stellar Spark clients on iOS and Android, making it a great tool for managing email across multiple devices.

Best utility apps

Alfred 4

Alfred 4+
Running with Crayons Ltd

★ ★ ★ ★ ★ 4.8 • 1.1k Ratings

Free

Alfred 4 is the latest and greatest version of Alfred, a better way to search for files on your Mac and the web at large.

But Alfred is more than a search tool: you can use it to launch apps, look up spelling and definitions, do quick calculations, and generally make the most of your new Mac.

The best part? It's free, though you can pay a one-time fee to buy a license and upgrade to a version with more powerful features, including the ability to play music from iTunes, create workflows and hotkeys, customize Alfred's look, and more.

Daisydisk

DaisyDisk is one of the best Mac disk space managers because it is powerful, flexible, and aesthetically pleasing. This $10 app will quickly scan your storage drives to show you a gorgeous interactive map of how your Mac's storage space is being used, and its drag-and-drop tools make it easy to quickly move files around and clear up some space. In addition, the most recent release now supports scanning drives on cloud storage services such as Dropbox, Google Drive, and others.

Meeter

Meeter for Zoom, Teams & Co [4+]
Join your next meeting faster
Bardeen Inc.

★★★★★

Free · Offers In-App Purchases

Meeter is a handy little app that sits in your Mac's menu bar and organizes all your video calls in one place, whether they be on BlueJeans, FaceTime, Google Meet, Microsoft Teams, Webex, Zoom, or about thirty other video-conferencing platforms.

In normal times Meeter is perfect for distant workers, but during the COVID-19 epidemic, it's a beneficial software for everyone who often jumps on video calls with family and friends.

The free version connects to your calendar and automatically pulls in details for your upcoming calls, making it easy to quickly see what you have coming up and join with a single click — no more rooting through your email to find the right meeting link.

Best Mac video or photo editing apps

CleanShot X

CleanShot X is a turbocharged screen-capturing tool for Macs, and if you spend a lot of time capturing pics or videos of your desktop it's a real-life-changer. The basic version costs $29 and gives you a more powerful suite of screen-capturing tools that make it easy to quickly snap a pic, edit or annotate it, combine it with other screenshots, and share it with whoever you need to via drag-and-drop. You can also record video of your screen (even while scrolling) with the option to capture your clicks, your keystrokes, or your webcam, then quickly upload that recording to the cloud or turn it into a GIF. Upgrade to the $8/month Pro version for unlimited cloud storage (the basic version gives you just 1GB), custom domain and branding options, and more.

Pixelmator Pro

Pixelmator [4+]
Pixelmator Team

#16 in Photo & Video
★ ★ ★ ★ ★ 3.7 • 893 Ratings

$4.99

Pixelmator Pro, which costs $40, is not the cheapest photo editing app on the App Store, but it is one of the best. As of this writing, it offers more than 50 image editing tools (including a full set of vector tools), including some pretty neat options like photo editing tools that tap into the power of machine learning. It's a strong competitor to Adobe Photoshop, with the added bonus that you only have to pay for Pixelmator Pro once, whereas

Adobe wants to charge you a monthly subscription fee to use its best photo editing tools.

iMovie

Apple's own iMovie isn't the most robust or professional video editor on the market (those honors go to expensive software like Adobe Premiere Pro and Final Cut Pro), but it's one of the easiest to use. Moreover, it is free, whereas the majority of full-featured video editors cost $100 or more. Since iMovie is Apple software it may well already be installed on your Mac, but if not, you can easily grab it from the App Store to do some quick video editing at up to 4K resolution.

Best Mac social media apps

Grids

Sure, you can log into Instagram via your web browser of choice, but it's not exactly the most ideal way to browse the image-sharing service. Enter Grids, a free app that makes browsing Instagram on your Mac a much more enjoyable experience. It has a good, clean design that loads quickly, and you can use it to view Instagram photographs and videos in a number of layouts. There's also a handy enlarged view mode for when you want to zoom in. Some of the standard Instagram features (such as the ability to direct messages to other users and view their stories) are only available in

Grids if you subscribe to the Pro version, which costs $2.50/month on a month-to-month basis or $1/month on an annual basis.

Tweetbot

If you use Twitter frequently, Tweetbot is a must-have app for Mac. This $10 app makes the experience of using Twitter much more enjoyable by giving you access to a powerful suite of filters that can help you block out spoilers, sponsored tweets, and more. It has a sleek user interface that makes it simple to track hashtags, switch between accounts, and add private notes to user profiles.

Best Mac entertainment apps

Spotify

Spotify - Music and Podcasts 12+
Discover the latest songs
Spotify

#1 in Music
★★★★★ 3.8 • 23.4M Ratings

Free · Offers In-App Purchases

If you're not already using Apple Music to kick out the jams, chances are good you're a Spotify user. Even if you aren't yet, Spotify makes it easy to set up a free account and start listening to your favorite musicians, and the macOS desktop client provides you more control over your playlists than the online app in a clean, easy-to-navigate interface.

Steam

Steam Link 17+
Stream Your Steam Library
Valve

★ ★ ★ ★ ★

Free

If you want to play games on your Mac, it's a good idea to download Steam. Launched by Valve nearly two decades ago, Steam has grown to become one of the biggest PC game platforms in the world. Not every game on Steam is compatible with macOS, but Steam makes it easy to filter through its 50,000+ games to see which ones run on Macs. There are lots of amazing options too, including everything from Sid Meier's Civilization VI and Stardew Valley to Cuphead, Hades, Disco Elysium, and more. Plus, you can connect a compatible Bluetooth controller for some old-fashioned gamepad gaming on your new Mac.

VLC

VLC media player 4+
VideoLAN

#35 in Photo & Video
★ ★ ★ ★ ★

Free · Offers In-App Purchases

If you need to play a video file but are uncertain whether Apple's QuickTime player will support it, VLC is the first media player you should download. It's one of the best media players on the market because it supports so many different types of multimedia, including DVDs, audio/video CDs, and file formats like Xvid, DivX, Real Video, and more—including Ogg Vorbis, a personal favorite. The best part? It's free, open-source, and available across multiple platforms, including iOS.

Chapter 5: Troubleshooting, Tips, and Tricks for Seniors

5.1 Use your Mac with other devices

Utilize a keyboard and mouse or trackpad on multiple devices with Mac's Universal Control

With Universal Control, you can work across up to three devices (for example, a Mac and an iPad) using a single keyboard and mouse or trackpad. Additionally, you can drag items between devices.

To utilize Universal Control, make sure of the following:

You're utilizing supported models of Mac and iPad.

Your Mac has macOS 12.3 or later, and your iPad has iPadOS 15.4 or later.

All of your devices are signed in with the same Apple ID using two-factor authentication using the same Apple ID.

You have Wi-Fi, Bluetooth, and Handoff switched on in System Preferences (on your Mac) and in Settings (on your iPad) (your iPad).

Connect your Mac to another Mac or iPad to use Universal Control

With Universal Control, you can establish a connection between your Mac and a nearby device, and then use a single keyboard and mouse or trackpad to work across the devices.

Note: If you haven't used Universal Control in a while, you may need to re-establish the connection.

Do one of the following:

1. Utilize your Mac's mouse or trackpad to move the pointer to the screen's right or the left edge. When a border appears at the edge of Mac's screen, the pointer must be moved past the border until it appears on the other device.
2. On your Mac, choose Apple menu > System Preferences, click Displays, click the Add Display pop-up menu, then choose a device below Link Keyboard and Mouse. Utilize your mouse or trackpad to move the pointer beyond the Mac's screen's edge until it appears on the other device.
3. On your Mac, click Control Center in the menu bar, click Display, then choose a device below Link Keyboard and Mouse. Utilize your mouse or trackpad to move the pointer beyond the Mac's screen's edge until it appears on the other device.

The direction in which you move the pointer while establishing the connection decides which side of the display you use to connect your devices. You can adjust this by changing the arrangement of the devices in Display preferences. Click on the image of the display, then drag it to the desired position.

You can set your Mac to automatically reconnect to any nearby Mac or iPad. Choose Apple menu > System Preferences, click Displays, click Universal Control, then select "Automatically reconnect to any nearby Mac or iPad."

Disconnect your Mac from another device

After you establish a connection between devices using Universal Control, the connection remains until either of the devices goes to sleep or you disconnect them.

On your Mac, open the Apple menu > System Preferences, then click Displays.

Select the device you wish to disconnect by clicking the Add Display pop-up option.

Turn off Universal Control

You can disable Universal Control to prevent your Mac from connecting to external devices in order to use a keyboard, mouse, or trackpad.

- On your Mac, open the Apple menu > System Preferences, then click Displays .
- Click Universal Control, then do one of the following:
- Turn off all Universal Control connections: Deselect the "Allow your pointer and keyboard to move between any nearby Mac or iPad" checkbox.
- Prevent a connection when moving the pointer to the edge of the screen: deselect the "Push through the edge of a display to connect to a nearby Mac or iPad" checkbox.

5.2 Talk to Siri

Siri on the Mac with macOS Big Sur delves much further into your program than it does on iPhone and iPad. It can search for files, examine your system settings, and understands contextual language, allowing you to ask a question and then immediately ask a related one.

How to activate Siri on Mac

When you initially set up your Mac or update to a new version of macOS, you will be prompted to enable Siri on your Mac. If you did not activate it initially, you may do it manually from System Preferences at any time.

- Click the Apple symbol in the upper-left corner of the display.
- Select System Preferences from the drop-down menu.
- Select Siri.

- To speak with Siri, check the box on the left side of the window.
- Select a language.
- Select a Siri Voice.
- If you don't want Siri to speak, turn off Voice Feedback.
- Choose either the internal Mic input or an external accessory for the Mic input.

How to activate "Type to Siri" on a Mac

In macOS High Sierra and later, you can type your search query to Siri instead of having to ask it out loud. So if you're in a meeting and your boss just asked you for a spreadsheet, you can ask Siri to retrieve it for you without interrupting the conversation.

How to activate Siri with a keyboard shortcut

You may access Siri through the app Dock or the Menu bar at the top of the display. But if you prefer keyboard shortcuts, you're in luck — Siri likes them, too.

- Click the Apple symbol in the upper-left corner of the display.
- Choose System Preferences from the menu drop-down.
- Select Siri.

Under Keyboard Shortcut, choose a keyboard shortcut to utilize. By default, you hold down Command-Space, but you can also choose Option-Space, Function-Space, or any other key combination of your choosing.

When a keyboard shortcut has been configured, you may press and hold the two keys until Siri appears.

How to use Siri on Mac with Airpods or supported beats headphones

If you have your AirPods or a set of Beats headphones that feature voice-activated Siri (currently just the Powerbeats Pro), you may call on Siri for help.

- Click the Apple symbol in the upper-left corner of the display.
- Choose System Preferences from the menu drop-down.
- Select Siri.
- Mark the Listen for "Hey Siri" on the headphones checkbox.
- If you want Siri to be activated by voice while your Mac is locked, select the Allow Siri when locked checkbox.

How to pin Siri results to the notification center

You can pin all Siri search results directly to the Notification Center. This may be quite useful if you need to keep track of documents for business, or if you want to add photos of Oscar Isaac to your Today display.

- To activate Siri, click the Siri icon in the menu bar or dock, or use the corresponding keyboard shortcut.
- Tell Siri to find you a file, or document, or perform a web search.
- Click the Plus (+) button next to the search results when they display in Siri's window.
- The results of Siri searches will be pinned to the Today view of the Notification Center. To delete it, hover over the search section of the Notification Center and click the X.

5.3 Back up your Files

You may have stumbled onto this page because you recently experienced the horrible scenario of your Mac failing without a backup, or because you know someone who has experienced such a tragedy and want to prevent it from happening to you.

Or perhaps you messed up a document you were working on, saved over something you didn't want to lose or realized you accidentally deleted a substantial amount of work. Recovering unsaved or lost Word documents might provide unique difficulties. If only you had a backup and could recover an earlier version.

Regardless of why you want to learn the best way to back up your Mac, we want to assist you in developing a backup strategy. We will examine the different types of Mac backups, such as local wired or wireless backups, live backups, remote backups, and online backup.

We'll also examine the best Mac backup solutions, including backing up to iCloud or another online service such as Dropbox, using Time Machine or other backup software for a local backup (we have an in-depth article about how to use Time Machine here), and the various remote backup services that are available to you if you want to make sure that you can recover your data if both your computer and local backup gets wiped out.

If you have just lost everything on your Mac due to a damaged drive, read this article for suggestions on how to retrieve your data from the damaged drive.

Ten reasons why you should back up your Mac

We're probably preaching to the choir here, but here are a few reasons why you should absolutely back up your Mac, in no particular order:

1. Because you (or another person) may accidentally spill a drink on your Mac.
2. Because your drive could fail and SSDs are notoriously difficult to recover data from.
3. Because you may lose your Mac or someone might take your Mac.
4. If you encounter Mac malware, a backup will allow you to retrieve your data before the infestation.
5. Before installing a major macOS update, you should back up your Mac in case something stops working and you need to revert to the previous version of the operating system.
6. You will be able to access old papers and previous versions of documents.
7. You may believe there is nothing on your Mac that needs to be backed up – perhaps you sync everything in iCloud – but we

promise you will miss something if you erase your Mac and expect to restore everything to its original state.

8. It makes setting up a new Mac very straightforward. You may quickly restore all your data onto a new Mac and continue as if it were the same computer.

9. It means you could access your data from another Mac if necessary.

10. Some things, like images, are difficult to replace or reproduce so be sure they are preserved carefully.

Best backup method for a Mac

There are numerous methods for backing up a Mac, but if you had to choose just one, which would you choose?

Time Machine, Apple's free backup software, is likely the easiest and most cost-effective alternative. The only related expense would be acquiring an external drive but given you can get 1TB storage for less than £40/$30 these days, it shouldn't break the bank. We've got a round-up of the best hard drives here.

Time Machine is an excellent backup option, but is it the best? A solution that is not stored in the same area as your Mac may be preferable, considering that a fire or water might destroy both your Mac and its backup.

There are other alternatives to Time Machine that you may find more suitable. We examine the finest backup software, including Acronis, ChronoSync, Carbon Copy Cloner, Carbonite, and SuperDuper, individually.

Option 1: Utilize Time Travel

Apple offers Time Machine, its own backup program, as part of macOS. It is a very user-friendly solution. Plug in an external storage device, such as a hard disk or solid-state drive, and begin Time Machine backups. We have a comprehensive guide for backing up your Mac with Time Machine.

Time Machine will generate a versioned backup of your Mac, which means it will save hourly backups for the previous 24 hours, daily backups for the previous month, and weekly backups for each month. You can thus retrieve a prior version of a document if necessary.

Not only does having a versioned backup protect you if something goes wrong with your Mac, but it also protects you against human mistakes (saving over a document for example). ChronoSync ($49.99/£36.00 at Econ Technologies) is also capable of creating versioned backups.

Additionally, Time Machine's strong integration with macOS is a plus. A Time Machine backup facilitates the transfer of all data, settings, and applications from one Mac to another. It is also really easy to use.

Time Machine's only significant drawback is that you must remember to connect in your hard drive, or else nothing will be backed up. However, you can set up Time Machine on a NAS drive for a wireless backup, but it may be a bit slower. You'll also need a substantial amount of storage because Time Machine incremental backups consume more space than the entirety of your Mac's data. We recommend utilizing a storage device with at least four times the capacity of your Mac. View our selection of the best hard drives.

How to create backups with Time Machine

Here is a step-by-step guide to backing up with Time Machine, but the essential steps are as follows:

- Connect hard disk or solid-state drive (alternatively you can use a NAS drive).
- You should notice an alert on your Mac asking if you wish to utilize the drive with Time Machine. Select Use as Backup Disk from the menu.
- If you do not notice the warning, ensure that the disk is formatted appropriately; it must be formatted as Mac OS Extended (Journaled).
- If you still don't see the notice, visit System Preferences > Time Machine and pick Backup Disk.
- Choose the storage device and click Use Disk.

Option 2: Use iCloud

With iPhones and iPads, you may use iCloud to save a backup of your device from which you can restore it. If you purchase a new iPhone, you may restore all of your settings and data using iCloud backup.

If you hoped to back up your Mac to Apple's iCloud instead of an external hard drive, you'll be disappointed: you can't back up your entire Mac to iCloud, and iCloud is incompatible with Time Machine. However, iCloud may still be utilized to back up a portion of your Mac's data.

You can automatically sync certain files from your Mac to iCloud; however, you should not consider this a backup, as there will be no previous version of the file if you delete or modify it. This is a synchronization, not a backup. However, having your files synchronized to iCloud is advantageous since you can access them from any Apple device (and even from a PC if you go via iCloud.com).

Included among the files that may be synchronized in this manner are all files on your Desktop and in your Documents folder. If you use applications such as Pages and Numbers, your documents will be saved to the cloud, and your Mail and Messages can also be kept in the cloud.

Apple requires a monthly membership fee for iCloud storage. Monthly subscription costs are as follows:

- UK: 79p (50GB), £2.49 (200GB), £6.99 (2TB)
- US: 99c (50GB), $2.99 (200GB), $9.99 (2TB)
- Euros: 99c (50GB), €2.99 (200GB), €9.99 (2TB)
- If you subscribe to Apple Music (£9.99/$9.99 per month), you can utilize iCloud Music Library to access your music from anywhere. Here, we distinguish between iTunes Match and Apple Music.

That's what you can sync automatically, but as we noted above, you can utilize iCloud to back up some of the data on your Mac merely by transferring it to your iCloud Drive.

Here is how to synchronize your Mac with iCloud.

- On your Mac, launch System Preferences and select iCloud.
- If you haven't already, sign in to iCloud.
- Check the box next to iCloud.
- Select the Options checkbox within the iCloud row.
- Check the box next to anything you want to keep in iCloud, including your Desktop folder, Pages documents, and System Preferences.
- How to make an iCloud backup of your Mac
- This will not be automated in the same manner as the sync, but it is a good idea to periodically copy any non-synced data to iCloud. This is how to accomplish it:
- Launch the Finder.
- Click on the iCloud Drive folder in the left-hand navigation bar.
- Open a second Finder window and search for any folders, files, or data linked with a non-cloud-based application.
- This information may now be copied to your iCloud Drive.
- Now you will not only be able to access the data on any of your Apple devices, and even via the web on a non-Apple device, you will be able to recover it if something goes wrong with your Mac. It is also an excellent method for obtaining an offline backup.
- Just don't forget to routinely update that 'backup'.

Option 3: Use a different cloud backup service

If you are looking for a way to sync and share files, there are numerous alternatives to iCloud. You could already be using Dropbox, Google Drive, Microsoft OneDrive, or one of the other Cloud storage options we look at here.

Rather than backing up all of your data, these solutions are typically employed for sharing files with coworkers or friends or storing files that everyone can collaborate on. You may subscribe to data plans that allow you to save all of your data in the cloud, similar to iCloud, but you would not be able to readily download a clone of your Mac if it were lost.

How to back up your files to Dropbox, OneDrive, or Google Drive

If you need to back up a few files, Dropbox, One Drive, or Google Drive may be a suitable option. You'll have the benefit of being able to view the files from any device and you will effectively have a low-cost off-site backup.

- In the case of Dropbox, sign up for an account on this page, then download and install the program. (Or sign in to your current account if you're already a member.)
- Once the program has been installed on your Mac, launch Dropbox to access the web interface where you may copy your files.
- Click Upload Files or Upload Folder on the right, go to the folder you wish to upload, and then click Choose. Wait while the folder uploads.
- Additionally, you may drag and drop your files and folders into Dropbox using the Finder. When DropBox is loaded on your Mac you will see a Dropbox tab under Favourites in the Finder, just drag and drop anything into that folder and it will be backed up to Dropbox, and available on any other computer or iOS device that has Dropbox installed.

The procedure is identical for all cloud storage services.

Option 4: Utilize a remote backup

There are specific online backup options, such as Carbonite, which will backup your Mac over the web for a cost ($4.92 per month, 15-day free trial). The aforementioned cloud services are more for synchronizing and sharing files than keeping all your data. Another alternative is CrashPlan for Business ($9.99, 30-day free trial).

The advantage of one of these dedicated cloud backup services is that the backup is remote, so if your Mac was destroyed in a fire or flood along with your Time Machine backup, you would still have a copy of all your data in a secure facility (these places will have a way of keeping your data safe and accessible even if they suffer a power outage or something similar, although we're not sure about the end of the world scenarios).

If you have internet connectivity and your Mac crashes, gets lost or is stolen, you can recover everything from this cloud backup.

There was a less expensive alternative than hiring a business to host your backup. Previously, it was possible to use CrashPlan for Home to sync your data to a drive at a friend's house, which significantly reduced the cost. Unfortunately, this service is no longer available.

The primary downside of any of these techniques is that it can take a long time to complete the first backup of your data, particularly if you have a sluggish internet connection, and it can also take a long time to recover all of your data — it might take weeks to restore all of your data. If you upload or download several hundred terabytes of data, you may exceed the upload and download limits of your internet connection and incur additional costs. You may also search for a provider that will offer you a backup drive that you can then submit to them for storage.

How to back up your Mac to a cloud-based storage provider

As with the alternatives to Time Machine outlined above, the manner in which you back up your Mac to one of these online services will depend on which one you select; nonetheless, the procedure is likely to go as follows:

- Sign up for an account with the service; you may be required to sign up for a subscription rather than making a one-time payment, as is commonplace today.
- Install the supplier-supplied software and complete the setup procedure.
- There's a chance that the backup procedure will start instantly. This might take Very Considerable Time. There may be settings in the app's Preferences that allow you to speed up the backup process, albeit the majority of the backup speed is governed by your broadband connection.

- Examine what is being backed up and deselect any unnecessary items.
- When the worst comes and you need to recover your data you'll probably need to log in with your ID and password – so make sure you save a duplicate of them somewhere other than on the Mac you are backing up.

Option 5: Clone your hard drive

As with Time Machine, you may use the backup disk – or clone – to restore your Mac in the event of a failure and to recover a previous version of a document or a deleted photo. In addition, just as with Time Machine, you must remember to connect in your external hard drive for the backup.

A clone differs from a Time Machine backup in that it can be booted from, so you could connect it to another Mac and boot up from it without restoring your Mac, which may be handy as an interim solution. You cannot use Time Machine in this manner.

However, recovering your Mac from a clone is no longer as straightforward as it once was. Beginning with Catalina and concluding with Big Sur and the introduction of the M1 Mac, Apple's organization of startup volume has evolved over the previous few years. Apple now divides the drive in half, isolating writeable data from the system volume (which is read-only and is where all your system settings and all the things macOS needs to work are stored). Not only is this system volume read-only, but it is also sealed, which means that if the seal is broken – which will occur if you attempt to boot from an external drive – the volume will be invalidated.

There are several solutions that backup software makers have devised to circumvent this issue, but recovering a Mac from a backup is not as dependable as it previously was, not least because Apple might alter things again, rendering your bootable clone obsolete. So recovering from a clone is no longer the best approach to recovering your Mac following a calamity.

Nonetheless, the data volume may be backed up. To accomplish this, you could use Disk Utility to copy the Data volume to a disk image or a drive.

How to duplicate a Mac

The method you use to clone your Mac will depend on the software you are using to back up your Mac, the Mac you own, and the version of macOS it is running – it may not be possible at all – but if your Mac is capable of creating a clone, you can expect something like the following:

- Connect your external storage device.
- You may need to format, or reformat, the drive before you can use it. In this scenario, launch Disk Utility, pick the external drive, click Erase, select macOS Extended (Journaled) from the list of available formats, then click Erase again.
- Launch your cloning program.
- It's possible that the program will give you an option to 'Copy' what's on your Mac's internal storage to the external disk. You will need to be mindful of what you may replicate - ensure that you copy all files, for example, otherwise your clone may not be bootable.
- Before the copy begins, you may be required to provide a password and confirm that you wish to delete all data from the external device.
- Expect the cloning process to take some time; when it is complete, click OK.

5.4 The Genius Bar for Troubleshooting your Mac

The Apple Store is a wonderful place to purchase Apple devices and accessories, but they may also assist with inquiries and repairs. The Genius Bar at the Apple Store is the official location to receive hardware-related support for Apple devices.

Let's examine how to schedule an appointment with the Genius Bar the next time you need one.

What Can the Genius Bar of Apple Help With?

The Genius Bar offers assistance with all accessible Apple products. They may assist with queries and issues regarding hardware and software.

However, certain repairs cannot be performed in-store. The Genius Bar must send your device out for some extensive repairs and computer screen repairs. The majority of simple phone repairs, including battery and screen replacements, may be performed in-store and returned to you the same day.

What Can You Repair at Home Without an Apple Appointment?

Depending on the issue you are having, there are a few basic solutions you may attempt before scheduling an appointment at the Apple Genius Bar.

Reboot Your Equipment

Restarting your computer should be your first line of defense against the majority of software errors and performance concerns. If your iPhone or iPad is unresponsive, restart it forcefully.

To forcibly restart an iPhone 8 or later: press Volume Up and let it go, press Volume Down and let it go, and then push and hold down the Side button.

To forcibly restart an iPad without a home button, press and release the volume up and volume down buttons, and then press and hold the power button.

Hold down the power button to forcibly restart a Mac.

Run Mac Diagnostics

If a conventional restart doesn't work, you can try rebooting your Mac in diagnostic mode by holding down the D key when you switch it back on. Your Mac will test its functionality and provide a diagnostic code that describes the problem.

Address Common Overheating Causes

If your laptop is overheating, there are a handful of fast remedies that could help. Adjust your surroundings, dismiss demanding tabs or apps, check the activity monitor, or reset the fan. If your phone is overheating, transfer it to a cool spot. In the summer, iPhones frequently overheat when left in hot automobiles or exposed to excessive direct sunlight.

Check Your Battery Health

Battery repairs are one of the most common fixes needed for Apple products. Check the health of your iPhone or MacBook battery to determine if it's time to replace the battery.

How to Book an Apple Genius Bar Appointment

Once you've established that you actually need to bring your device into the Genius Bar, follow these steps to book an appointment:

- Visit Apple.com on your computer or mobile device.
- Select the Support option from the main menu.
- Choose Apple Repair
- Select Start a Maintenance Request
- Select the type of equipment for which you require an appointment. Select the category (iPhone, iPad, Watch, etc.) followed by the device model.

The website will highlight many kinds of device-related concerns. Choose the issue you're experiencing.

The site will then provide the option to send in the device, locate a nearby approved service provider, or schedule an appointment at the Genius Bar. To schedule an appointment with the Genius Bar, choose "Bring In For Repair."

It'll ask you for the serial number of the device if relevant, or to choose the device from the registered devices on your Apple account. If you need assistance discovering the serial number for any Apple product, please see our tutorial.

The site will now provide venues nearby where you can bring your device. To assist you in deciding where to go, their earliest appointment availability is displayed.

Choose your preferred Apple Store location and available appointment time from the list provided.

Resolve Problems with Your Apple Device by Scheduling an Appointment

The Genius Bar is an excellent resource for resolving Apple hardware issues. There is a multitude of repair methods for typical issues such as cracked displays and dead batteries. The Genius Bar can assist, but many customers prefer to perform repairs themselves or visit local businesses. Consider the risks and benefits of each alternative.

Bonus: Mac Keyboard Shortcut

I'm sure the majority of Mac users are aware that Command-C means copy and Command-V means paste, but there are a multitude of additional shortcuts that make life easier for Mac users. I've compiled the following examples to show this truth:

Esc

Never underestimate the Esc key's ability to get you out of trouble. Say you're taking a screenshot and managed to choose the part of your screen for that shot, only to learn it's the wrong section - touch Esc and you won't need to worry about it. That is essentially the Esc principle. Use it to cancel a prior command. Another example is a web page won't load and is sucking up your system resources?

Command-W

Closes the window that is presently active. Option-Command-W closes all active application windows.

Command-Y

Numerous individuals utilize QuickLook to preview products they are interested in. To utilize QuickLook, pick an item in the Finder and hit the space bar to display a preview. Select an item (you can even use the Up and Down arrows to navigate to it in Finder view) and then press Command-Y.

Command – Period (,)

This is one of the lesser-known Mac keyboard shortcuts, but it's really handy. You are working on an application, and you wish to see the application's preferences. You may browse to the menu bar and scroll through to view the preferences if you so want. Alternatively, you can press Command-, (comma) to access them as quickly as possible.

Command-G

I am certain that you utilize Command-F to locate objects, such as words in a document or on a website. Command-G is its lesser-known cousin. Utilize it to traverse through each occurrence of the desired object. This implies that if you use Command-F to locate all instances of "Command" on this page and then press Command-G, you may traverse through each one. Oh, and you can also press Shift-Command-G to return to the previous screen.

Command-M

This combination minimizes the front application window to the Dock, whereas Command-Option-M minimizes all front application windows.

Option and Direction

If you cannot view your desktop for all the open programs, click anywhere on your desktop while holding down Command and Option. You may just wish to access all open windows for a certain application; in this instance, hold down the same keys and click on any open window for that application.

Command-Shift-A

Select this combination when in Finder/Desktop view to access the Applications folder, or substitute the A with U to reach the Utility folder (or D for Desktop, H for Home, or I to access iCloud Drive).

Command-Space

The combination of Command-Space activates Spotlight; simply press and hold these keys and begin entering your query. (I suppose you already know about Command-tab?)

Command-L

The quickest method to do a search or browse to a website in Safari, Command-L quickly chooses the address bar: begin entering your query, then use the up/down arrows to select the right option.

Command-Tab

While holding down Command, launch the program switcher and use Tab to browse to the desired application.

Command-Option-D

Show or hide the dock from most applications.

Fn-left arrow (or right arrow)

Using the function key and the right (to the bottom of the page) or left (to the top of the page) arrows, you may quickly go to the top or bottom of a web page. You can accomplish the same result by pressing Command-Up or Command-Down. Utilize Control-Tab and Control-Shift-Tab as a third option.

Command-left/right arrows

Hit Command and the left arrow to go back to a page in the browser window. Press Command Right to continue going.

Tab nav

Use the Command-Shift-] and Command-Shift-[characters to navigate between different tabs.

Command-Shift-\

The simplest way to view all open tabs is within a single Safari window.

Option-Shift-Volume

Option Shift plus volume up/down allows you to adjust Mac's volume in tiny increments. Option Shift may also be used to adjust the display's brightness by tiny increments. Learn further Option secrets here.

Fn twice

To launch Dictation on your Mac, press the function (fn) key twice, then begin speaking, and press fn again when you're finished. Here are some additional suggestions for using your voice to control your Mac. Nota bene: macOS Catalina now includes the significantly more potent Voice Control, which allows you to control everything on your Mac using only your voice. Learn more about this topic here.

Option-File

Option when choosing the File menu in Safari provides access to the 'Close Other Tabs' command. Try the other Safari menu items with Option depressed to find other commands you probably weren't aware of.

Optional Brightness Boost (or down)

Utilize this command to launch preferences fast. Or, press Option in conjunction with the Mission Control or Volume (up/down) buttons to access the Mission Control and Sounds preferences.

Command – Backslash

This is one of the lesser-known Mac keyboard shortcuts, but it's really handy. Use this combination to navigate between open windows in the active application. You'll wonder why you hadn't utilized it earlier.

Command - Control - Space

Want to include emoji and other symbols in your writing? Control-Command-Space will bring up the Character Viewer, where you can select and use these symbols.

Command-P

Do you open a document before printing it using the File menu? Do this instead: Select the document in Finder and click Command-P. The item will open, and the Print dialogue will display. You may also use Command-P to print the current item in the majority of applications.

Option + Command + Esc

In the event that an application freezes or hangs, you can force quit it by pressing Option-Command-Esc. Sometimes, a simple program restart is all that's required to get your system back up and running.

Command + Management + Q

Leaving behind your Mac? Tap this keyboard shortcut to lock your computer immediately.

Touch Bar hint number 1

If you use a MacBook Pro with the Touch Bar, you may press Shift-Command-6 to grab a picture of what is on your Touch Bar. Want to get a picture to insert into the document you're typing in? Simply press

Control-Option-Command-6, and the image will be copied to the clipboard.

Touch Bar tip No. 2

This MacBook Pro Touch Bar hint is especially helpful if you frequently hit the Siri button by accident: you can alter the button's location so you are less likely to do so. Choose to customize the control strip in Keyboard Preferences. Observe the Touch Bar, and you will notice that the icons are slightly unsettled. Move your pointer to the bottom of your screen and continue going (as if you were moving it off the screen); one of the touch bar items should be highlighted. Now, put your pointer on the Siri button and then drag and drop it a couple of spaces to the left.

Touch Bar hint number 3

Utilize the function keys often in some applications. Obviously, you may access them by hitting the 'fn' key. However, the Touch Bar may be configured to always display the function keys in such apps. To accomplish this, visit Keyboard System Preferences, choose Function Keys, and press the plus sign (+). Then you may choose the app (s). If you wish to perform a standard Control Strip command while using one of the applications, just press Fn to return to that view.

Safari tips

There are several keyboard shortcuts for Safari:

- Command + I: Open a new email message with the page's content.

- Command + Shift + I: Open a new email containing merely a page's URL.
- To shift your window down one screen, use the spacebar.
- Shift+Spacebar: Moves the window one screen higher.
- Command + Y: Open/close the History window.
- Option + Shift + T

This online browser trick can sometimes be a lifeline. When conducting research, Command + Shift + T will open your last closed tab, which is quite useful if you accidentally close a window without preserving the UR.

Conclusion

It is not a secret that the elderly are getting more tech-savvy and gaining access to the same technologies as the younger generation. The most recent Office of National Statistics (ONS) report on internet usage revealed that the number of older people using the internet has continued to rise, with 47% of those over the age of 75 and 83% of those between the ages of 65 and 74 being recent users.

So, it's excellent that a growing number of elderly individuals have realized the potential of computers and the internet. However, it is important to keep in mind that elderly users may require more assistance with setting up and maintaining their computers—and this is where local technical support comes into play.

Are Macs superior for the elderly?

We won't revisit the old Mac vs. PC discussion in this article, but there are several reasons why Macs are a great option for older users:

- They are simpler to install.
- They're easier and more intuitive to use
- They're more protected
- They sync effortlessly with other Apple gadgets including iPhones, iPad, HomeKit, and other devices
- Their integrated software is perfect for simple picture and video editing. Many customers choose Macs because of their satisfaction with the Apple ecosystem, which makes it simple to attach their iPhone or Apple TV to their Mac for file sharing and content synchronization. For older users, it makes sense to stay within one ecosystem to avoid confusion and compatibility difficulties, but help may still be required on occasion.

Made in the USA
Monee, IL
24 January 2023

26031684R00069